Acknowledgments

CW01499692

This book was written during the COVID-19 pandemic in 2020–22, when time away from the domestic sphere was scarce. In writing a book that is so engaged with Virginia Woolf's insistence that writers (of all genders) have a quiet space and a door that locks, I am not immune to seeing the humour in the way that COVID-19 made writing this text more challenging. I owe a debt of gratitude to my family, who allowed me the chance to escape into the mountains and deserts of California for weeks of thinking and writing when that was not possible at home. The first draft of this book began on Anacapa Island in the Channel Islands National Park and the book was completed in the boulders of Pioneertown in the High Desert.

On a personal level, the support that Heather Sheaffer, Hannah McSwiggen, and August Sheaffer have provided has been instrumental to the way that this book has taken shape. Long-winded philosophical conversations and collaborative artmaking with Aaron Michael Smith (occasionally serving as writing breaks) keeps me going when time seems too heavy. Warmth from Niki, Manny, and Duke – the lap-loving cat and dogs in my life – has given me hope for continuing benevolence in interpersonal existence, even in the midst of a global crisis that has us all feeling so deeply isolated.

Thanks are due to Jamie Hook, Eric Zobel, Hannah McSwiggen, Heather Sheaffer, Aaron Michael Smith, and Ashley Allen for their insightful and gracious feedback on drafts (and drafts, and drafts) of the chapters contained herein. Hannah McSwiggen also acted as an informal research partner on this book, helping to comb through SP-ARK and isolate changes between screenplay drafts. Grace Byron provided a much-appreciated entrance point to my writing, sending along the listing for the photographic exhibition Swinton curated. I am grateful to Garrett Chaffin-Quiray for being willing to share his teaching experience with me. I also want to extend thanks to my collaborators on the film *Playland* for their patience while I split my time between producing and writing.

Having the chance to ruminate on a single film for such an extended period has been a unique gift. I am grateful to Thomas Waugh and Matthew Hayes for their vision, criticism, and support throughout this process. My thanks also go to Jonathan Crago, Kathleen Fraser, and the whole team at McGill-Queen's University Press, whose guidance has made this text stronger at every turn.

On an institutional level, this book was written with the support of Palomar College. I would like to extend specific thanks to Candace Rose and Wendy Nelson for their continued support of my teaching, research, and creative work.

ORLANDO

Queer Film Classics
Edited by Matthew Hays and Thomas Waugh

The enduring commercial success of LGBTQ2I films over recent generations offers proof of widespread interest in queer film within both pop culture and academia. Not only are recent works riding the wave of the new maturity of queer film culture, but a century of queer and proto-queer classics are in busy circulation thanks to a burgeoning online queer cinephile culture and have been brought back to life by omnipresent festivals and revivals. Meditations on individual films from queer perspectives are particularly urgent, unlocking new understandings of political as well as aesthetic and personal concerns.

Queer Film Classics at McGill-Queen's University Press emphasizes good writing, rigorous but accessible scholarship, and personal, reflective thinking about the significance of each film – writing that is true to the film, original, and enlightening and enjoyable for film buffs, scholars, and students alike. Books in the series are short – roughly 40,000 words – but well illustrated and allow for considerable depth. Exploring historical, authorial, and production contexts and drawing on filmic analysis, these open-ended essays also develop the author's personal interests or a subjective reading of the work's sexual identity discourses or reception. The series aims to meet the diversity, quality, and originality of classics in the queer film canon, broadly conceived, with equally compelling writing and critical insight. Books in the series have much to teach us, not only about the art of film but about the queer ways in which films can transmit our meanings, our stories, and our dreams.

L'Homme blessé
Robert Payne

Boys Don't Cry
Chase Joynt and Morgan M Page

Orlando
Russell Sheaffer

ORLANDO

Russell Sheaffer

McGill-Queen's University Press

Montreal & Kingston | London | Chicago

© McGill-Queen's University Press 2022

ISBN 978-0-2280-1459-1 (cloth)
ISBN 978-0-2280-1460-7 (paper)
ISBN 978-0-2280-1570-3 (ePDF)
ISBN 978-0-2280-1571-0 (ePUB)

Legal deposit fourth quarter 2022
Bibliothèque nationale du Québec

Printed in Canada on acid-free paper that is 100% ancient forest free
(100% post-consumer recycled), processed chlorine free

Unless otherwise noted, all figures are © 2012 Sally Potter/Adventure
Pictures.

Library and Archives Canada Cataloguing in Publication

Title: Orlando / Russell Sheaffer.
Names: Sheaffer, Russell, author.
Description: Series statement: Queer film classics | Includes bibliograph-
    ical references and index.
Identifiers: Canadiana (print) 20220275106 | Canadiana (ebook)
    20220275149 | ISBN 9780228014607 (softcover) | ISBN 9780228014591
    (hardcover) | ISBN 9780228015703 (PDF) | ISBN 9780228015710 (EPUB)
Subjects: LCSH: Orlando (Motion picture) | LCSH: Potter, Sally, 1949-—
    Criticism and interpretation. | LCSH: Gender identity in motion pic-
    tures.
Classification: LCC PN1997.O74 S54 2022 | DDC 791.43/72—dc23

Contents

Synopsis

Sally Potter's *Orlando* follows its titular character through four hundred years of British history. Played beautifully by Tilda Swinton, Orlando begins their journey as a young nobleman sitting below an oak tree in 1592 – a "feminine" person in appearance, but a "young man" all the same. Quickly winning the affection of Queen Elizabeth (played by controversial gay icon Quentin Crisp), the Queen tucks the deeds to Orlando's family estate in Orlando's garter. After the death of the Queen, Orlando courts Sasha, the daughter of a Muscovite ambassador, during the "great frost" of 1610, which has turned the River Thames into a frozen playground for the wealthy.

Although often seeking companionship, Orlando faces frequent challenges fostering meaningful, long-term connections with people, moving from relationship to relationship (sometimes romantic, sometimes intellectual) while remaining in love with literature and poetry. The film makes frequent time leaps through the use of simple title cards, moving from 1600 to 1610 to 1650 to 1700 to 1750 to 1850 and then finally to an undated present (the moment of the film's making in 1992). Aside from Orlando, most of the film's characters do not reappear across multiple time periods.

Orlando's sense of self is challenged when they encounter the threat of violence while serving as an ambassador in Khiva, Uzbekistan, in the 1700s. Asked to take up arms against "mutual enemies," Orlando is forced to reconcile their peaceful, poetry-loving sense of self with their understanding that propelling oneself into battle is a fundamental element of being a man. Rather than join the battle, they enter one of many extended slumbers. Waking up seven days later, Orlando has transformed into a woman. Looking in the mirror at their naked body, Orlando famously brushes off the change; "Same person. No difference at all. Just a different sex," they say. Returning to their family estate in the United Kingdom, they are informed that, as a woman, they are no longer entitled to their family estate.

After falling in love with an American explorer (Shelmerdine, played by Billy Zane), a now pregnant Orlando jumps forward in time, stumbling through a battlefield (thereby signalling the passing of the two world wars) and landing in the 1990s with a daughter. Orlando finishes a manuscript for *The Oak Tree*, a book that they have been working on since they were a young man in 1592, and receives praise from a prospective publisher. Orlando, with helmet on and daughter by their side, rides a motorcycle back to their old family estate. Sitting under the ancient oak tree that they were beneath at the beginning of the film, Orlando's daughter moves around the scene, filming Orlando with a small handheld video camera. Orlando looks up to see an angel floating in the sky, singing to them from far above the oak tree.

Credits

Orlando, 1992, UK/Russia/Italy/France/Netherlands, 94 minutes
Adventure Pictures presents a co-production with Lenfilm, Mikado Film,
  Rio, and Sigma Filmproductions with the participation of British Screen

Director: Sally Potter
Produced by: Christopher Sheppard
Co-producers: Roberto Cicutto, Jean Gontier, Matthijs Van Heijningen,
  Luigi Musini, and Vitaly Sobolev
Writer: Sally Potter, based on the book by Virginia Woolf

Cast
Tilda Swinton: Orlando
Billy Zane: Shelmerdine
Lothaire Bluteau: The Khan
John Wood: Archduke Harry
Charlotte Valandrey: Sasha
Anna Healy: Euphrosyne
Heathcote Williams: Nick Greene / Publisher
Quentin Crisp: Queen Elizabeth I
Peter Eyre: Mr Pope
Thom Hoffman: King William of Orange

Kathryn Hunter: Countess
Ned Sherrin: Mr Addison
Jimmy Somerville: Singer / Angel
Dudley Sutton: King James I

Crew
Director of Photography: Alexei Rodionov
Editor: Hervé Schneid
Original Music: David Motion and Sally Potter
Music Supervisor: Bob Last
Production Design: Ben Van Os and Jan Roelfs
Costume Design: Sandy Powell
Additional Costume Design: Dien Van Straalen
Casting: Irene Lamb

Distributed by Sony Pictures Home Entertainment

Made with the assistance of the European Co-production Fund (UK)

Developed with the support of the European Script Fund, an initiative
of the media program of the European Community, and the National
Film Development Fund, London, England

Premiered as a part of the official competition at the Venice Film Festival
in September 1992

Nominated for Academy Awards for Best Art Direction and Best Costume
Design

ORLANDO

Introduction
Orlando as they/them
(on the queerness of Sally Potter's *Orlando*)

I first found a DVD of Sally Potter's *Orlando* (1992) at a now-defunct video store near my graduate school apartment. I became enamoured quickly. Tilda Swinton's performance, Sandy Powell's costumes, and Sally Potter's temporal fluidity all made so much sense as I was beginning to understand my own queer-theoretical perspective for the first time. Ruminating on the film just over a decade later, I am struck by how intellectually and aesthetically seductive I continue to find Potter's work, especially with regard to non-normative understandings of both bodies and time.

When I teach the film in my Introduction to Cinema classes, however, I am often surprised by how troubled straight-presenting, mostly male students are by the film. A cursory reading of the film's synopsis points to the areas of greatest bafflement: each time we come to the moment when Orlando is seen in the nude – now "female," although previously "male" – with Tilda Swinton's naked body fully visible, I hear a collective, masculine "what?!" After screening the film in my classes, questions tend to abound: was Orlando always a woman? And does she really live for hundreds of years? What *is* this film about? Regularly suspending their disbelief for the newest superhero film, these students nevertheless stumble when I suggest they consider *Orlando* as they might any other fantasy film. If Orlando was ever a woman, their questions seem to suggest, she must have always been a woman.

In anecdotal discussions with colleagues, it is clear to me that this level of confusion pervades other professors' classes as well. While "most students" agree that the film is "sumptuous," Garrett Chaffin-Quiray has noted to me that "the titillation of nudity" often "gives way to recognition of a rather antiseptic bit of scopophilia that is disturbed with Orlando telling us what to know/how to feel about [their] transformation" from male to female. This discomfort stems equally from the film's form as well as its subject matter: students find the film "slow and strange" while simultaneously struggling to accept the way that "behavioral changes" concerning gender and embodiment have varied "across time and across cultures." In short, the film "can require lots of contextual work before you really get into the movie" (Chaffin-Quiray, email to author, 30 December 2021).

The discussions that manifest when I teach the film in my Queer Cinema course, however, tend to be quite different. Instead of remaining fixated on the moment of Orlando's nude reveal, we frequently end up in larger conversations about fluidity (historical, sexual, and formal). While some queer cinema students do struggle with the film as a period drama – which seems to be a challenging cinematic form across the board – frustration with Orlando's morphing relationship to gender is infrequent. Instead, my students often understand the film in terms of trans and nonbinary experiences. These disparate encounters teaching *Orlando* continue to remind me of the topical, structural, and evolving queerness that sparked my adoration of *Orlando* in graduate school.

Soon after I prepared the proposal for this book, I received an email from a fellow queer artist (and former student) who had also been struck by the beauty of *Orlando*. Knowing my love for and fascination with Sally Potter's film, she pointed me towards an exhibition of *Orlando*-inspired photographs that was set to tour in 2019 and 2020. The exhibition ran at the Aperture Gallery in New York from May to July 2019, followed by installations at Literaturhaus in Munich and the McEvoy Foundation for the Arts in San Francisco. Curated by Tilda Swinton, the exhibition featured "recent and newly

Figure 1
Photographer Collier Schorr documents the transition of model Casil McArthur from "boyish girl to girlish boy." Photograph by Deyane Moses of Aperture's *Orlando* exhibition. Photograph courtesy of Deyane Moses, *Aperture* magazine, 303 Gallery, and Collier Schorr.

commissioned photographs inspired by the themes of Virginia Woolf's prescient 1928 novel, which tells the story of a young nobleman during the era of Queen Elizabeth I who lives for three centuries without aging and mysteriously shifts gender along the way" ("Exhibition" 2020). With an eye for collage, colour, and (of course) gender play, Swinton's curatorial logic highlights the ways in which the film continues to resonate with audiences.

A special edition of *Aperture* magazine highlights much of the photographic work from the exhibition – diverse in its voice and approach – with essays that pull the work back towards the themes of *Orlando* as both novel and film. In their discussion of Collier Schorr's portraits of model Casil

McArthur, "who transitions over the course of a multiyear project from boyish girl to girlish boy," Jack Halberstam highlights the ways that Tilda Swinton's performance in Potter's *Orlando* "represents a kind of apex within a visual history of androgyny." Intertwining the film's interest in gender ambiguity with the way that androgyny "flickers in and out of style" in fashion, Halberstam notes that there has been a "recent focus on transgender bodies in popular culture" that speaks to a move away from "his/her clothing and towards the concept of they/them" (Halberstam 2019, 56). The change in Casil's appearance that we can see in Collier Schorr's stunning portraits is, like Orlando's own, a slow one that requires our "patience" as we witness the internal made visible.

Antwaun Sargent notes that painter and photographer Mickalene Thomas's portraits for the exhibition, featuring models of colour in "ornate suits and beautiful gowns," work to provide a "fresh embodiment of Woolf's amorphous vision," mapping the iconography of British colonial portrait painting onto the bodies of black femmes. In so doing, Thomas's portraits allow her subjects to be "cast desirously" while also highlighting the ways in which "passing" (with regard to both race and embodiment) is a "giv[ing] up" of the self. "Passing," Sargent explains, is "something black women, femmes, and anyone existing outside of whiteness have had to rebel against, both racially and sexually, in an effort to claim space for survival and power, to make the world sensitive to their realities." The question posed by Sargent – "is [passing] worth it when so much of the self has to be given up to exist in tradition?" – is one that productively extends the thematic concerns of Potter's film, finding intersectional resonance a century after Woolf's writing and decades after the release of Potter's film (Sargent 2019, 134).

A morphing text that – to my mind – is at once feminist and queer, Potter's *Orlando* certainly grapples with the politics of "passing" and of gender while simultaneously being about British history and histories of embodiment, about our imaginations and fantasies, about language and image, about time and stasis. As our international understanding of queerness, queer bodies,

Figure 2 Top
Potter directs Tilda Swinton on the set of *Orlando*.

Figure 3 Bottom
Potter directs Quentin Crisp on the set of *Orlando*.

and queer subjectivities continues to develop, Potter's *Orlando*, which adapts Virginia Woolf's 1928 novel of the same name, seems eternally relevant with new and repeat audiences continuing to see themselves in Potter's vision.

Moving slowly and lingering on extended glances of Orlando at different moments throughout their life, the film highlights shifts in gendered performance across time. Where Woolf's book is more explicit in its description of Orlando's occasional same-sex relationships, Potter's film is far less overtly lesbian in terms of Orlando's same-sex attraction. But the film, meditative in its flow, also revels in ambiguities. The audience is never given definitive answers as to how Orlando has lived so long (or why) and how their sex has shifted mid-film. The audience is also never provided clarity as to how or when a relationship might be defined as romantic, sexual, creative, or intellectual. This purposeful ambiguity leaves the film open to opposing interpretations, with some scholars understanding it as markedly queer or – as others have argued – as quite the opposite. This bifurcation in perspective is rooted in the fact that Potter's most obvious alterations from Woolf's novel included the erasure of the most straightforwardly lesbian elements.

In the thirty years since *Orlando*'s release, many modes of queer identification have made moves away from past investments in identity politics – which often emphasized binary desire and difference as a tool of lesbian and gay visibility – and towards an embrace of self-identification, androgyny, and fluidity. This shift has allowed for an ever-expanding range of LGBTQ+ subjectivities to gain public legibility, providing new vocabulary and nuanced models for queers of all ages. In this blossoming landscape of potential nonnormative becomings, *Orlando*'s multitude of prospective readings have helped it feel continually more relevant and, in my argument, more queer.

Since its premiere, Potter's *Orlando* has had a rich life in repertory screenings, has been described as a central companion piece to the Met Costume Institute's *About Time* (a 2020–21 exhibition),[1] and was a part of an interdisciplinary performance work titled *Orlando: The Queer Element* in 2017. A collaboration between BFI Flare (the British Film Institute's LGBTQ+ film festival) and Clay & Diamonds (a group of educators and theatre makers in the UK who "explore humanity and strengthen our communality through open and frank collaborations between artists and scientists"), "Orlando: The Queer Element" functioned as an educational tool to get students thinking about gender and sexuality by placing Potter's film alongside live performances from actors. The "live cinema event," describes Clay & Diamonds, "played with what it means when we call ourselves 'woman,' 'man' and those spaces in between" (Clay & Diamonds). At once fodder for artists and educators, it is striking how relevant Potter's film remains decades after its initial release. In the words of a *Vogue* headline from November 2020, "Nearly Three Decades Later, Sally Potter's *Orlando* Is More Topical Than Ever." Writing in the heat of the 2020 presidential election, Laird Borrelli-Persson notes that "in fashion and society, gender fluidity is a topic that is becoming increasingly talked about. Yet what struck me most in rewatching the film in an election year notable for its vitriol and grandstanding is how stereotypes of masculinity – and its links to strength, power, and force – remain entrenched in (American) society. The bravado expected of Orlando as a man in the 17th century seems to be on display daily in the 21st-century news" (Borelli-Persson 2020). This link between stereotypical attributes of masculinity ("grandstanding," here) is topically key to Potter's film; Orlando's own change in sex is interwoven with a "crisis of masculine identity," which occurs when they are asked to enact violence at the film's mid-point. Articles including Borrelli-Persson's highlight the way that Potter's *Orlando* remains a part of mainstream conversations about sex, gender, and embodiment through its representation of identity that is complex and multifaceted.

Called a "gorgeous banquet" by the *Washington Post* (1993) and "a triumph of intelligent, lyrical yet argumentative film making" by Caryn James for the *New York Times* (1993), Potter's *Orlando* was also celebrated in its moment of release. Vincent Canby's remarks in an earlier review for the *New York Times* seem especially prophetic now: "*Orlando* could well become a classic of a very special kind, not mainstream perhaps, but a model for independent film makers who follow their own irrational muses, sometimes to unmourned obscurity, occasionally to glory" (1993). Potter's adaptation as well as the performances of Tilda Swinton (as Orlando) and Quentin Crisp (as Queen Elizabeth I) were given noteworthy praise upon the film's theatrical release. "An early scene in the film pairs a young Orlando with the ailing queen," a review in the *Washington Post* explains. "They lie down – a woman playing a man, a man playing a woman – close to each other in bed. 'I wanted to sort of turn it on its head so at the very beginning there already were question marks all over,' Potter says" (*Washington Post* 1993). Those "question marks," perhaps a detriment in the hands of a less-skilled adapter/director, are a large part of what made *Orlando* so thrilling to audiences and critics upon its release in 1993 and they are also a part of how the film has been taken up so queerly in the decades since.

Potter's adaptation, however, is not without critics. While Potter's oeuvre has repeatedly been described as feminist – and we should consider *Orlando* an example of that – Potter herself has a complex relationship to that term. Potter has articulated concern regarding framing her work as "feminist," despite her work having been consistently viewed, reviewed, and described in those terms. In an often-cited interview from 1993, Potter attempts to articulate that she does not find it productive to assume that her voice as a woman will somehow manifest as fundamentally womanly on screen. An artist who has, time and again, worked to push back on a logic that equates female filmmakers with "women's cinema," Potter explains in the interview that, with regard to understanding her work as "feminist": "[I] can't use the word any more because it's become debased. My simple observation is that if I use it, it stops people thinking. They close down. There is a small inner circle, of course, for whom it has a different meaning, but in general usage it seems to cause more problems than it solves. So I now try to find more subtle ways, more indirect or appropriate ways to the individual or the circumstance to express some of those ideas – which in any case have moved on ... And anyway language needs to keep refreshing itself perpetually" (Florence 1993). Reading her responses in this interview, it strikes me that Potter is not fighting against the logic of "feminist theory." Instead, she is attempting to place her work in line with theories and histories of gender and feminist thought without hitting the wall of anti-feminism, where conversation breaks down the moment the word "feminist" is used. Elsewhere, Potter has yearned to just be considered a "filmmaker" instead of a "feminist filmmaker"[2] – and that desire is certainly understandable, especially given the longstanding practice of pigeonholing "women's cinema."

Critical of Potter's work, Susan Watkins writes that the film (and Potter as a director, more generally) struggles with the language of identification and embodiment. Watkins notes that Potter, who doesn't understand her work as "feminist," also does not see her film fitting within the "great queer wave" because "it is about a more polymorphous sexuality rather than specific sexual identities. I don't think the book so much explores sexual identities as dissolves them" (Watkins 1998, 53). Watkins's interpretation of Potter's statement, though, needs historical context. At the moment of *Orlando*'s release, when the interview was conducted, the "great queer wave" that is discussed would have been another description of an emergent "New Queer Cinema." In 1992 (the year before *Orlando* screened at the Sundance Film Festival), in an article written for the *Village Voice* and reprinted in *Sight & Sound* magazine, film critic B. Ruby Rich described an explosion of "new queer cinema" that was allowing for the development of specifically gay male voices at Sundance (Rich 2004). This "New Queer Cinema," though, was one that centred mostly around gay male stories and directors while sidelining narratives about and by queer women.[3]

It is not surprising, then, that Potter hesitates to conceptualize her film within the realm of this new burst of queer content, what Penny Florence calls the "Great Queer Wave" and Rich calls "New Queer Cinema." After all, as Florence mentions in her question to Potter, "in the 'Great Queer Wave,' women are conspicuous by our absence" (Florence 1993, 282). Given that the films in this blossoming "New Queer Cinema" often relied on firm identity categories,

Potter's note that the film "is about a more polymorphous sexuality rather than specific sexual identities" is an astute observation. Where Watkins understands "Woolf's performative understanding of gender identity [to allow] space for a feminist politics which acknowledges and attacks women's oppression," it is within this decentring of identity categories that Watkins understands there to be "something disturbing about the implications of Potter's belief in an essentially gender-free self" (Watkins 1998, 54). Watkins's argument may have been quite salient in the years following *Orlando*'s release when lesbian and gay identification was a political tool for the community. The way that young, "queer" identified individuals have engaged with issues of categorical identification over two decades later, however, troubles Watkins reading of Potter's film.

Ruminating on Potter's *Orlando*, I am struck by how queer I find the film to be, how obviously it has been taken up in relation to our current use of the term "queer," and – at the same time – how much I feel like the lack of same-sex scenes makes me feel that I need to rationalize the film as a "queer film classic." It is hard to get away from the fact that Potter's adaptation transforms a novel with literal same-sex relationships (Woolf's *Orlando* features multiple sexually inflected relationships between women) into a film that is much more queerly about time and embodiment, ultimately removing the titular character's same-sex relationships from the diegesis altogether.

Reading through the range of scholarly responses to Potter's film, it is clear that some do not embrace Potter's film as a revolutionary queer text. In Potter's reworking of Woolf's book, we certainly see a move away from the source material that had been taken up within lesbian feminist politics,[4] changed instead into something much more diffusely about "queerness." For scholars who hold Woolf as an icon of lesbian (or bisexual) feminism, this shift is often troubling. Leslie K. Hankins argues that "Potter's treatment of *Orlando* represents a 'heterosexualized betrayal of a lesbian love letter'" in so far as "the lesbian presence in the film is conspicuous by its absence" (Fowler 2009, 62). Hankins's note is crucial: Woolf's text was famously written as a love letter to

Vita Sackville-West. Writing to Vita to ask "if she would give her permission to be the subject of this unusual biography, Vita replied on 11 October 1927," saying, "My God, Virginia, if ever I was thrilled and terrified it is at the prospect of being projected into the shape of Orlando. What fun for you; what fun for me ... You have my full permission" (Piggford 1997, 53–4). The resulting novel is one that is invested in a loving fictionalization of nonfiction details. Woolf pulls large details from Sackville-West's life, of course, but she also includes details about Orlando's estate that are pulled directly from records regarding Vita's childhood home of Knole; these details are as minute as the colour of Orlando's chairs (Baldanza 1955, 274–9). In one of the most quoted accounts of Woolf's novel, Sackville-West's son (Nigel Nicolson) writes that "the effect of Vita on Virginia is all contained in *Orlando*, the longest and most charming love letter in literature, in which she explores Vita, weaves her in and out of the centuries, tosses her from one sex to the other, plays with her, dresses her in furs, lace and emeralds, teases her, flirts with her, drops a veil of mist around her, and ends by photographing her in the mud at Long Barn, with dogs, awaiting Virginia's arrival next day" (Nicolson 1973, 202–3). This move away from the lesbian (or "sapphic" in the language of Woolf's era) elements was one that Potter was conscious of at the time of the film's release. In a press interview timed with the theatrical release of *Orlando*, Potter told Penny Florence that "there is the fact that the book draws on, at its core, Virginia Woolf's love for another woman, Vita Sackville-West. I think that feeling of love is in the film. I think, however, just as Virginia Woolf took a step away from her source material, which is really what Vita was, and transformed Vita's life into a novel, the film takes several steps away from the book" (1993, 282–3).

These "steps away from" the same-sex relationships that are both within and behind the scenes of the novel are understandably troubling for critics who want to understand Potter's film as an extension of the lesbian-rich world of Woolf's text. For Watkins, "Woolf's novel is much more ambivalent – and thus more radical – about gender identity, than Potter's film, partly because Woolf unharnesses theories of gender identity from any specific feminist agenda and partly because the novel medium is more conducive to such flexibility" (1998, 42–3). These moves away from Woolf's source text, however, situate *Orlando* firmly within the topical interests of Potter's oeuvre.

Potter began her career as a choreographer, performance artist, and experimental filmmaker. An early short film of hers, *Thriller* (1979), reimagines Puccini's *La Bohème* with rich feminist critique. Potter's first feature film, *The Gold Diggers* (1983), featured Julie Christie in what *Sight and Sound* described as a "feminist sci-fi musical extravaganza." *The Gold Diggers* was savagely critiqued in the press, resulting in Potter's near-decade break from narrative feature filmmaking, which ultimately ended with the release of *Orlando* (1992). Looking back at the arc of Potter's early and middle career, it is now clear that *Orlando*'s romantic couplings are aligned with those of Potter's later films. Over the course of her career, Potter has proved to be a director whose work often grapples with the gendered (and political) elements of heterosexual relationships. This interest in the dynamics of heterosexuality has continued to pervade Potter's career: she has directed seven narrative features between 1992 and 2021, four of which revolve around conflicted heterosexual relationships.[5]

I believe, however, that Potter's "gender-free" sensibility in *Orlando*, while certainly eschewing lesbian-specific interpretations and standing apart from the "New Queer Cinema" that B. Ruby Rich was describing in 1992, is one of the crucial components of the film that embraces its own distinct queerness, especially in the ways that the term has come to be used two and half decades after the film's release. Film scholar So Mayer argues that, in Potter's oeuvre, "cinema is celebrated as an art form capable of making change because it incorporates all the arts without losing its specificity" (Mayer 2009, 3). I would add that, although the conflicts in Potter's films often centre around language and naming, her cinema allows for the nonverbal – the spaces and glances between the words – to be radical.

To my mind, it is Potter's fluid, visual imagining of Woolf's text that allows the film to refocus the novel's queerness. Potter moves away from Woolf's direct narrative investment in same-sex relationships and towards an embrace of the queerness inherent in cinematic time and performance. This, I argue, is a large part of why we might consider Potter's *Orlando*, with its lack of diegetic same-sex relationships between its characters, to be a "queer film classic." This argument, I know, may be a stretch for some and downright disagreeable to others. Embracing an understanding of queerness that decentres sex is a political move that stands apart from the identity politics driven Gay Rights movement that led to the films of the 1990s, but it's one that is in the process of blossoming out in our current queer world. Taking inspiration from adaptation theory and the work of Alexander Doty, I have assembled this book as a series of close readings. In so doing, I hope to point to the ways that we might embrace *Orlando* as a queer film classic, even as we celebrate Woolf's *Orlando* differently – as a lesbian or bisexual literary classic.

The format of my text is broken into three chapters. In the first chapter, I take a methodological cue from Doty and provide a close reading of the film itself, focusing on the couplings (all heterosexual – at least on the surface) as a way to understand queerness as about far more than sex.[6] Because issues of adaptation have been so central to understanding the politics of Potter's film as either queer or not (or lesbian or not), the second chapter of this book examines four of Potter's screenplay drafts leading up to the published script for the film, all of which Potter has made available online through her own archive (called SP-ARK). By examining the four drafts side by side, it is possible to map the way that Potter approached Woolf's text, moving from a strict adaptation to one that embraces Potter's own unique (and political) voice, pushing Woolf's text past its canonical ending point. In so doing, I argue that Potter's drafts illuminate the trajectory by which her version of *Orlando* embraces the queerness of time and embodiment, even if we might call the film's lack of engagement with same-sex relationships into question. In framing this chapter, I take particular inspiration from Pamela Demory's note that "adaptation theory is already queer" insofar as the discipline centres on the way that adaptations are promiscuous with regard to their source material, resisting "singular definitions" (2019, 3). And, finally, my third chapter works to understand Potter's film alongside the more theoretical aims of Woolf's body of work, explicitly tying Potter's *Orlando* to Woolf's *A Room of One's Own*.

Before diving into a close reading of Potter's *Orlando*, I also feel it necessary to clarify my use of language with regard to the character of Orlando. Scholars have used varying pronouns to think about Orlando, often choosing to identify Orlando with he/him/his pronouns when Orlando is in the "male" phase of life and she/her/hers pronouns when Orlando is in the "female" phase of life. This is the approach that Potter has used in interviews and how Orlando is identified in Potter's scripts and in Woolf's novel. With that in mind, when quoting the script or another source, I have left the author's chosen pronouns for Orlando intact. In my own descriptions of Orlando, however, I have elected to use they/them/theirs pronouns. In our current queer world – and especially because *Orlando* has been taken up as a "kind of apex within a visual history of androgyny" (Halberstam 2019, 56) – third-person singular pronouns provide a particularly productive avenue by which to think holistically about the way that Orlando moves as an individual across or outside of gender throughout the film. To my mind, although Potter's film engages productively with binary gender, it positions Orlando as existing outside of (or at least troubling) that dynamic. I hope that by electing to use they/them pronouns for Orlando, this text can continue to foreground and celebrate *Orlando*'s role in social conversations regarding nonbinary representation.

Chapter 1

the body trapped in ice
(close reading Potter's *Orlando*)

For a film that features a total lack of same-sex relationships within its diegesis, Sally Potter's *Orlando* is a strikingly queer film and is continually becoming more so. This, I think, stems from the film's palimpsestuous nature. On the surface, we're given a narrative with a three-act structure that navigates through nearly four hundred years of British history through the eyes of the fictional, ageless Orlando (Tilda Swinton). At the beginning of the film, we are told that the young, aristocratic, male Orlando, although "heir to a name that meant power, land, and property," is far more interested in the pursuit of "company" than "privilege." Waking up mid-film as a woman, Orlando loses the rights to their home and property (eliminating the location of their "privilege"), but they also never quite succeed in finding the diegetic "company" they seek. While the film's fluidity with regard to, and critique of, gender has been readily apparent to scholars and critics, its representation of queer relationships has proved ambiguous to some and dubious to others.

This relationship to queerness stems, in large part, from the fact that when Orlando is a man in Potter's film, they desire romantic relationships with women. When they are a woman, they fall in love with a man. In narrative terms, then, the explicitly romantic relationships in Potter's *Orlando* follow strict heterosexual lines. In one of the fiercer indictments of the film, Leslie K. Hankins writes that the film espouses a logic that says, "it's all right to change sex, as long as you end up with a heterosexual couple between the sheets" (1995, 176). Yet, from the very first moments of the film, we are faced with a barrage of blockages to understanding the film in heteronormative terms. Namely, the film invites numerous layers of subversion to its own narrative arc:

- The film embraces Tilda Swinton and Quentin Crisp's star images as gender ambiguous and queer, inviting us to get lost in the space between the characters on screen and the bodies of its actors.
- The film sets up an interest in "company" above romance in the voiceover that begins the film, blurring the lines between the kinds of relationships Orlando seeks and why.
- The film's playful engagement with time invites us to think cyclically as it continually jumps forward. Thus, when Orlando is proposed to mid-film (as a woman), the audience is forced to reconsider Orlando's past relationships with women.
- And the film actively engages with Woolf's source text – a novel (written as a faux biography) which *does* feature same sex romantic relationships and was written as a love letter to Vita Sackville-West (which I discuss at length in chapter 2 of this book).

By layering together all of these facets of heteronormative subversion, the film comes to embody what June L. Reich termed "genderfuck" (1992) – a sense of self that destabilizes our understanding of queerness as fundamentally about identity politics.[1]

In this chapter, I take a methodological cue from queer film scholar Alexander Doty, providing a close reading of the film itself. To do so, I have focused on the couplings around which *Orlando* is structured (all heterosexual – at least on the surface), using these close readings as a way to understand queerness as extending beyond simply an interest in sex. Specifically, this chapter examines Orlando's relationships with themself, Queen Elizabeth I, Euphrosyne, Sasha, Nick Greene, the Khan, the Archduke Harry, and Shelmerdine. I end this chapter with a rumination on another of the film's relationships, that between King James and a peasant woman locked in suspended animation. Although a break from the focus on Orlando's relationships, this last close reading allows for an exploration of the way that cinema itself manifests Queen Elizabeth I's demands on Orlando: cinema makes queer relationships to time and age possible.

THE BOY, THE ANGEL, and THE QUEEN

Gender fluidity is central to the opening of Potter's *Orlando*. In the first moments of the film, the audience sees Tilda Swinton's famously androgynous body beneath an oak tree. As Orlando gazes passively away from the camera, we are told via voiceover that "there can be no doubt about *his* sex despite the feminine appearance that every young man of the time aspires to." If the audience makes it no further, they have been immediately faced with a queer sort of quandary: is this performance a form of drag? Are we to read the performance as intentional cross-gender casting? Film scholars Karen Hollinger and Teresa Winterhalter have argued that Swinton's image is "transparently female, as the male Orlando," which creates an understanding of her presence on screen as "parody or comedic Shakespearean cross-dressing" (2001, 240). For theorist Jackie Stacey, "only a partial passing is intended" (2015, 259). So Mayer takes this a step further, arguing that once the femininity of Swinton's body is revealed, "it is even more troubling" than it was in its "male" form (2008, 42). While I do see room for understanding Swinton's performance as a form of longing for a queer embodiment in which a heteronormative masculinity is decentred, Hollinger, Winterhalter, and Mayer's points are well taken – Swinton does not pass as heteronormatively male and that poses an intellectual "troubling" for *Orlando*'s audience. For those viewers familiar with Swinton's oeuvre, these issues of embodiment require a further series of complex negotiations. Are we to shutter our knowledge of extratextual Swinton as a "female" actor who often approaches issues of gender in her work? If so, are we intended to unquestioningly embrace the notion of Swinton's Orlando as a "young man"?

These are issues of casting and stardom that Potter is acutely aware of. In her book *Naked Cinema: Working with Actors*, Potter writes that, for "well-known actors," "audiences will confuse the role with the actor, or the way they look with who they inherently are" (2014, 12). This is in accord with film theorist Richard Dyer's argument that we understand our stars across time and discrete films. Dyer writes that we understand "the roles and/or the performance of a star in a film ... as revealing the personality of the star" (1986, 22). While the star themselves, the filmmakers who employ them, and the industry professionals who support their star image all have a hand in how we publicly perceive these actors, Dyer also makes the observation that "the audience is also part of the making of the image. Audiences cannot make media images mean anything they want to, but they can select from the complexity of the image the meanings and feelings, the variations, inflections and contradictions, that work for them" (2004, 4).

We do not understand what it means to be "Tilda Swinton" (the individual) nor what it means to be a "Tilda Swinton film" (Swinton's oeuvre) in isolation apart from the larger web of representation from which we understand the star herself. When we watch a movie, we can only ever understand it from our present moment; we cannot detach ourselves from our extra-filmic knowledge. As such, audiences are constantly recoding and reunderstanding films, making meaning from infinite future moments that diverge from the one in which a film was shot. Thinking in 2022 about Swinton's role in *Orlando* (shot in 1991), it would be disingenuous for me to argue that I can separate out Swinton's performance in *Orlando* from her roles in Derek Jarman's *Caravaggio* (1986) and *Edward II* (1991) (both of which were released before *Orlando*). Similarly, writing in 2022, I cannot separate out Swinton's performance in *Orlando* from her roles in *Blue* (Derek Jarman, 1993), *Adaptation.* (Spike Jonze, 2001), *Broken Flowers* (Jim Jarmusch, 2005), *The Chronicles of Narnia* (Andrew

Adamson, 2005), *I Am Love* (Luca Guadagnino, 2009), *We Need to Talk About Kevin* (Lynne Ramsay, 2011), *Moonrise Kingdom* (Wes Anderson, 2012), *Only Lovers Left Alive* (Jim Jarmusch, 2013), or any of the other nearly ninety projects of which she has been a part.

Making the intertextual queerness explicit, Swinton spoke about the intersections of her performances, collaborations, and identity for a February 2021 British *Vogue* cover story. Asked about the way that her career was made by "working primarily with queer people," Swinton notes that she came out of the experimental theatre scene, then finding her community at the British Film Institute. In that world, she met "Derek Jarman, Peter Greenaway, Sally Potter, [and] Peter Wollen. But I'm very clear that queer is actually, for me anyway, to do with sensibility. I always felt I was queer – I was just looking for my queer circus, and I found it. And having found it, it's my world." In this statement, Swinton's reference to a queerness of "sensibility" is one that, to my mind, echoes *Orlando*'s own. This sensibility, as many popular publications explained in the wake of the British *Vogue* article, is one that encompasses both her explicitly LGBTQ+ roles – the "androgynous angel Gabriel in *Constantine* … the Ancient One – who was a Tibetan man in the comics – in *Doctor Strange*" and her role in "the boldly sexual *Female Perversions* opposite Amy Madigan in the 1990s" – and those that we might understand as simply "weird" (Rude 2021).

While Swinton's fame and presence in popular culture have only grown since the release of Sally Potter's *Orlando*, she was already well known at the moment of the film's release, particularly as a frequent collaborator with queer filmmaker and painter Derek Jarman. Her link with Jarman and, specifically, her role as the face of his film *Edward II*, which had been released in 1991 (roughly a year before *Orlando*), cannot be understated. In interviews for *Edward II*, Jarman noted that the role was a direct "revolt" against Swinton's own history. "Tilda grew up with British royalty," Jarman told the *Los Angeles Times*. "She went to school with Lady Diana – and she's in full revolt against all that. Her family is probably the oldest in Britain; 36 generations of Swintons, since

780, have lived in the same castle. I suspect her portrayal is a sort of revenge on that sort of world" (Thomas 1992a). Although *Orlando* had been in pre-production for years at the point *Edward II* was released, its impact on interpretations of Swinton's performance in *Orlando* are undeniable. These two period pieces, released a year apart, both featured Swinton involved in a rewriting of British history, establishing Swinton as a performer with, as theorist Jackie Stacey has argued, a "reputation as a figure whose presence belongs to the project of contesting historical narratives and the traditional chronologies and teleologies that have anchored them" (2015, 253).

Gender play also quickly became a part of the public conversation about Swinton that circulated in the press for her films. By the time Swinton starred in *Orlando*, she had already played men on stage and screen, a frequent detail in news articles about the actor around the time of *Orlando*'s release. In 1993, the *New York Times* noted that Swinton had "portrayed men twice before: she was once Mozart in the play 'Mozart and Salieri,' and in a one-woman show called 'Man to Man.'" When asked if she'd have preferred to be born a man, Swinton responded that she had "no complaints ... but I don't know that if someone came in now and shouted, 'All women leave the room,' if I would immediately leave. I would much rather say, 'Exempt!'" (Pener 1993). This play with the politics of gender is in accord with Stacey's argument that "Swinton's persona has become associated with her love of crossing conventionalized gendered boundaries" (2015, 259).

These elements of a revisionist mentality towards history – both Swinton's own personal history and British history more generally – and of Swinton's gender-playful persona were key elements of the publicity campaign that aided *Orlando*'s release. In many ways, the way that *Orlando* was positioned through this campaign has worked to establish the androgynous, gender-playful star persona of Swinton that has become so celebrated over the last two decades. To return to Potter's note that for "well-known actors," "audiences will confuse the role with the actor, or the way they look with who they inherently are" (2014, 12), we must therefore acknowledge that the way in

Figure 4
Tilda Swinton in *Man to Man* (directed by John Maybury, 1992). Photograph by
Liam Daniel. Courtesy of and © Basilisk Communications.

which audience members read films intertextually is often encouraged by the
publicity campaigns that bring those same films to theatres in the first place.
In the case of *Orlando*, the intertextuality of Swinton's own burgeoning (and
now abundant) star image – centred around timelessness and androgyny –
only enhances our potential queer readings of the film. Alongside her supporting cast (particularly Quentin Crisp and Jimmy Somerville), the film actively encourages us to think queerly about our young protagonist in the first
moments of the film.

As we reach the end of *Orlando*'s opening credits, night has fallen. Orlando
is asleep under the oak tree, pen in hand. They awaken frantically and rush

back to their home. In wide shot, we see torch-bearing servants rushing from the doors of the home on a strikingly grand estate. With a swish pan, Orlando runs against the stream of servants, towards their home. The mood is frantic. We see oars "[cut] rhythmically into the dark river water" while a high falsetto sings "in honour of Queen Elizabeth I" (Potter and Woolf 1994, 4). In this moment, we see Jimmy Somerville, the high falsetto we have been hearing, singing in a beautiful close-up. Somerville, the unmistakable voice of the 1980s pop bands Bronski Beat and the Communards, was an out gay figure for a decade before *Orlando*'s release. Our first images of Somerville feature him adorned in glittering gold with shimmering earrings and a halo-like crown. The telephoto lens refracts the similarly auburn light of the torches behind him, creating a moment in which Somerville's presence is at once angelic and haunting.

A signal that our queer ship has come in, Somerville's presence is quickly punctuated by a similarly glittery telephoto close-up of Queen Elizabeth I (played by Quentin Crisp, "who once described himself as 'England's stateliest homo'" [Thomas 1992b] and has been described by Potter as the "Queen of Queens" [Florence 1993, 283]). With an abnormally abundant amount of head room that allows us to take in all of her headpiece's glittery glory, we see the Queen in the dark and in profile. As the Queen exits the boat, we see her move away from the camera; a mysterious, stately presence has arrived, ushered into the scene by Somerville's queer falsetto. "The flow of ambiguities across these three figures," writes theorist Jackie Stacey, "stages gender as a series of queer impostures: Swinton as woman playing a young nervous, boyish aspiring poet; Somerville as a lavishly adorned soprano … Crisp … is in full regalia as the all-powerful but aging female colonial Monarch." With this queer trinity foregrounded in the first moments of Potter's film, in the words of film scholar Cristina Degli-Esposti, the audience is "immediately conscious that the story will be about inferences, contradictions, exceeded limits, and (possible) metamorphoses" (1996, 84).

Back inside the Great House, Orlando is breathing nervously, hastily being fitted for the formal attire that they should have been in hours ago. As the Queen walks slowly into the manor, Orlando hurls their now properly dressed body forward towards their duties and their queen. Orlando grabs a bowl of rose petal water, kneeling to offer it to the Queen, who dips her ring-heavy hands into the bowl in an extreme close-up. As Vivian Kao notes, "as we watch the hands dip themselves into the rosewater, we expect … to be able to deduce a body from a hand. But the next shot we see turns out not to be the face of the Queen, nor even the face of a woman, but the unmistakable mug of Quentin Crisp disguised as the Queen" (2015, 286). While I would argue that the film positions Crisp *as* the Queen and not *disguised as* the Queen, Kao's note that a history of "stately film and stately homes cannot be separated from its 'stately homos'" is well taken. In a film whose music and lyrics are narratively significant,[2] Kao notes that Somerville's song during the Queen's processional references "Eliza, the fairies' queen" which we might read as positioning "Crisp as the 'queen' of the 'fairies'" (2015, 286).

Like with Swinton, the extratextual star power of Crisp colours our reading of his role as Queen Elizabeth I. At the time of *Orlando*'s release, Crisp had hit a peak of notoriety as a controversial figure in gay culture. His first autobiography, *The Naked Civil Servant*, had been made into a television movie in 1975 (directed by Jack Gold), catapulting the then-sixty-seven-year-old to a form of pop stardom. In Crisp's words, "the teleplay in which I had appeared for about a minute and a half [Crisp appears in the film's introduction] came to be called my program. This was not because my presence was in any way dramatically effective but, because, from being constantly photographed, my image became recognizable – as unchanging as a stuffed bird, though not as silent – an object of ridicule to schoolboys and of curiosity to taxi drivers" (Crisp 2000, 292). Dyer notes that "a star image consists of what we normally refer to as his or her 'image,' made up of screen roles and obviously stage-managed public appearances, and also of images of the manufacture of that

Figure 5
Quentin Crisp as Queen Elizabeth I, "Queen of the Fairies."

'image' and of the real person who is the site or occasion of it" (2004, 7). Crisp's image came to stand in for popular representations of gay men in a way that is, in the logic of Richard Dyer's theorization of film stars, deeply intertwined in the messy relationship between film roles (specifically in *The Naked Civil Servant*) and the audience's understanding of Crisp as a "real" person.

This understanding of Crisp as the singular image of gay men was a step backwards for many gay activists, as ACT UP founder Larry Kramer explained to the *New York Times* in 1997. "Quentin Crisp has never fought for us or for the cause," Kramer explained. "He's been fighting for himself, for the right to wear a strange outfit down the street. I actually find him embarrassing, because the world, which doesn't see gay men, thinks he's the representative gay man, which makes it harder for us" (Witchel 1997). With decades of retrospect, both Crisp's statements – which were published with headlines like "'Stately Homo' Backs Call to Abort Gay Babies" (Kennedy 1997) – and Kramer's condemnation of Crisp as overly effeminate (or "strange") are deeply troubling.

During his life, Crisp repeatedly spoke to the intersections of performance, representation, and identity; his writing is littered with references to his own conscious performance of self and the need to remain "calculated" (Crisp 2017, 27). The film version of *The Naked Civil Servant* begins with Crisp on screen, made up in his now iconic look that was once described as an "older, contemporary version of the New Yorker's signature image, the dandy Eustace Tilley" (Thomas 1993). Directing his gaze straight at the audience, Crisp says: "When the people came to me and said 'we should like to make a film of your life,' I said 'yes, do. Films are fantasies. Films are magical illusions. You can make my life a fantasy as I have tried and failed to make it.' Then they said 'we want the film to be real. You know, real life.' So I said, 'any film, even the worst, is at least better than real life.' Then they said, 'though of course we should have to have an actor to play you.' I said, 'I have spent sixty-six years on this earth, painfully attempting to play the part of Quentin Crisp. I have not succeeded. Yes, of course you must have an actor to play me.'" In these first moments of the film, Crisp echoes Richard Dyer's concerns regarding the intersections of star image and the "real" person who is an actor on screen (or is Dyer echoing Crisp?). The realms of star persona and "real" life, of course, are joined even closer by the fact that *The Naked Civil Servant* was a work of autobiography. While Crisp was famously played by John Hurt in both *The Naked Civil Servant* and, later, in *An Englishman in New York* (directed by Richard Laxton, 2009), Crisp managed to foster his own image over the course of the two decades that followed *The Naked Civil Servant*'s release, although his performance of self was inevitably bound in the public consciousness with Hurt's representation of him.

When it came to acting in Potter's *Orlando*, Crisp "didn't prepare at all … [he] simply said the words as though [he] meant them" (Crisp 2017, 131). "I could only lend my gracious presence to a film," Crisp writes in his second autobiography. "I could never play a part. Who would I pretend to be?" (2000, 322). Crisp, clearly, was a guiding force in the collision of his own star persona and "real" life – a collision that Sally Potter harnesses in *Orlando* as a way to reimagine the imperialist British state (embodied by Queen Elizabeth I) as one of England's most famous, androgynous figures. Embracing Quentin Crisp's star persona at the time of *Orlando*'s release, Potter's film recodes British history. With Crisp's identification as a trans person later in life,[3] this representation takes on even more complex meaning – a personal "fantasy," perhaps, in the way that Crisp describes in the opening of *The Naked Civil Servant*. Those who do not know Crisp's life or work at all are still greeted, as Vivian Kao notes above, with a surprising directorial decision regarding gendered performance – one that forces us to acknowledge our own assumptions about gender and history.

Seated at dinner in an extravagant banquet hall, Crisp's Queen is adorned in gold, seated on a gold throne, and flanked by Orlando's mother and father in a wide shot. Signalled by their father, Orlando recites a section from Edmund Spenser's *Faerie Queene*, touching on the way that the queen "fades and falls away," but is quickly interrupted by the Queen, who asks if this is a "worthy topic from one so clearly in the bloom of youth, to one who would desire it still?" Orlando's father placatingly rationalizes Orlando's selection by noting that the Queen's "bloom is legendary." Taken together, these first moments of the film establish a clear portal through which the audience is invited to think intertextually. With *The Naked Civil Servant*'s immense popularity, many knew details of Crisp's own sex life. By reading Quentin Crisp's own "bloom" into the character he[4] plays, the audience is again invited to fill the textual space that resides between the actor and the character, making Queen Elizabeth I a queer figure.

Out for a walk around the estate, the seemingly contentious relationship between Orlando and the Queen quickly turns to affection. Signifying what film theorist Glyn Davis has described as a queer "changing of the guard" from one generational "form of otherness" to the next (2016, 162), the Queen straps a garter to Orlando's thigh, saying "I want you here in England with me. You will be the son of my old age and the limb of my infirmity. My favorite. My mascot." Later, in her bedroom, the Queen invites Orlando into bed with her. As Orlando "tentatively clambers up beside her," their face is "[buried] in her lap" (Potter and Woolf 1994, 8). Removing a rolled parchment from her bodice, the Queen tucks it "sensuously" into Orlando's garter (Potter and Woolf 1994, 9). "For you and for your heirs," says the Queen, "the house." "But on one condition. Do not fade. Do not wither. Do not grow old."

Queerness abounds in this encounter and in the myriad ways we might read it. We could understand these moments of intergenerational sensuousness between the Queen and Orlando in at least the following ways:

- as a heterosexual coupling between the Queen (a woman) and Orlando (a young man). Or,
- as a heterosexual coupling between Quentin Crisp (at the time of production, culturally understood as a "man") and Tilda Swinton (a "woman"). Or,

Figure 6
Queen Elizabeth tucks the deeds to the home into Orlando's garter.

- as a queer coupling between Quentin Crisp (at the time of production, culturally understood as a "homosexual man") and Orlando (a young man). Or,
- as a queer coupling between the Queen (a woman) and Tilda Swinton (a woman). Or,
- as a queer coupling taking into account the actors' star personas between Quentin Crisp (a famous entertainer who came out as a trans woman late in life) and Tilda Swinton (a famous and frequently androgynous actor).[5]

The range of ways we might read this relationship is only further complicated by Crisp's own, very public, very vocal proclamations that he "gave up sex at thirty" (Crisp 2017, 15). If we are to understand *Orlando*'s Queen as an extension of Crisp and Crisp as a self-proclaimed and very publicly "asexual" person (Crisp 2017, 5), then we can pull away from seeing the encounter between the Queen and Orlando as sexual in nature. Here, this sensuous (as opposed to sexual) encounter between Orlando and the Queen is as much a generational and imperialist transfer of property as it is a transfer of queer power. When the Queen tucks the deed into Orlando's garter, we see someone who has been locked into the identity categories of the gay liberation movement passing along a queer legacy to someone who has become an icon of androgynous performance that transcends binary categorization.

How we read Crisp's presence and body in the film is a question much in line with how we read Swinton's – do we accept the narrative placement of these gendered entities? After all, like the articulation of Orlando as unquestionably male in the first voiceover of the film, Crisp's character is undeniably female. As film scholar Cristina Degli-Esposti argues, although Crisp and Swinton may be in drag as actors, their characters are not within the diegesis of the film (1996, 86). Whether we suspend our disbelief and actively engage with these characters on the film's terms or read these characters intertextually, we are forced to make personal decisions about how we are going to understand these characters. As is evident in Kao's reading of the Queen's introduction, Crisp's casting is anything but neutral – we are meant to question the body on screen.

EUPHROSYNE and SASHA

The first of Orlando's explicitly romantic relationships that we encounter is their coupling with Euphrosyne (played by Anna Healy), which begins at the end of the era marked as "1600." Just after the funeral for Orlando's father, we see Orlando standing in front of a painting of their parents. In wide shot, Euphrosyne approaches Orlando's side to comfort them in "his time of grief." Orlando looks to the painting, then to Euphrosyne. Taking Euphrosyne's arm, Orlando turns them both to look straight into the camera, mimicking the painting's positioning of Orlando's parents and signalling that, through death, an exchange of power has occurred. With Swinton's signature flat affect,[6] there is nothing about this coupling that implies love or pleasure – this is a coupling full of assumptions; one made by habit. While this relationship does not last long (we almost immediately see Orlando flirting with another woman), Potter manages to give her audience a slight, knowing, inversion: standing in front of the portrait, Potter places Orlando and Euphrosyne in inverse placement to the positioning of Orlando's father and mother; Orlando stands in front of his mother, Euphrosyne stands in front of Orlando's father. Describing this swap in placement as "clearly parodic," film and gender scholars Suzanne Ferriss and Kathleen Waites argue that the portrait provides "a clear reference to the gender confusion at the heart of the Orlando's relationship with Euphrosyne" (1999, 113). While the (heterosexual) relationships on display in this moment of *Orlando* may look conventional, something is just different enough to undermine the familiarity of the classical family portrait.

Immediately after this *tableau vivant*, we jump forward in time: two title cards read "1610," "LOVE." While we might expect the warmth of youthful attraction, we're greeted with an icy scene: the River Thames has frozen over and Orlando and Euphrosyne skate along its icy surface towards a tent full of distinguished guests. Although Potter's film has us assume that the couple's relationship has lasted for about ten years,[7] Orlando and Euphrosyne have only been romantically linked for about one minute of screen time. Almost immediately after the "LOVE" chapter has begun, we are introduced to Sasha (played by Charlotte Valandrey), "the daughter of the Muscovite Ambassador," who – literally – makes Orlando's jaw drop. Orlando abandons Euphrosyne on the ice, making it clear that, despite its temporal link to the beginning of

Figure 7
Orlando (played Tilda Swinton) and Euphrosyne (played by Anna Healy) stand in front of a portrait of Orlando's parents.

Orlando's relationship with Euphrosyne, the title card that starts this chapter of the film refers to a new romance with Sasha.

We are then thrown into an icy love triangle. Orlando, who begins spending the bulk of their time with Sasha, has clearly displeased Euphrosyne along with a host of older women who, shouting across the ice, remind Orlando that Sasha is "a foreigner." Orlando's friends also encourage Orlando to break off the romance with Sasha. "My Lord Orlando," says the Earl of Moray (played by Simon Russell Beale), "you're in danger of becoming a fool ... don't you see, in courting a Cossack, you're humiliating not only your fiancée, but the entire female population of this country?" Taking off her engagement ring and throwing it to the icy floor, Euphrosyne stares Orlando down, proclaiming that their actions are an example of "the treachery of men." Turning towards the camera after Euphrosyne storms off, Orlando rationalizes their actions to the audience. "It would never have worked," Orlando tells us, "a man must follow his heart." In these moments, we see a break from tradition – Orlando would rather follow their heart than the trajectory that family and country have set out for them.

In Potter's hands, though, this quest for "love" is not uncomplicated and Orlando's romance with Sasha is also short lived. Thinking they see Sasha in the arms of a sailor, Orlando pleads with Sasha to stay with them forever. "Our destinies are linked," opines Orlando, "you're mine!" Sasha, who has clearly drifted from reciprocating Orlando's affections, simply responds, "why?" "Because I adore you," Orlando responds naively and possessively. While Potter directs Swinton to deliver these lines in earnest, the audience winces at Orlando's understanding of adoration equalling ownership; it is a logic rooted in the colonization of bodies through institutional romance. When Sasha, after Orlando desperately tries to get her to agree to run away with them, fails to meet them "at midnight under the London Bridge," Orlando looks straight into the camera and echoes Euphrosyne's earlier line, declaring that Sasha's actions are an example of "the treachery of women." Although undoubtedly empathizing with Orlando's pain, the audience is encouraged to side with Sasha in her rejection of them and their imperialist masculinity. Orlando may be genuinely infatuated, but they are also clearly falling into a masculinist trap, perpetuating a logic that the film/Potter finds unproductive.

Although Orlando accuses Sasha of "treachery," the film encourages the audience to understand Orlando as the "treacherous" character in their love triangle with Sasha and Euphrosyne – fault with regard to the dissolution of both relationships is attached solely to Orlando. In David Natharius and Bethany A. Dobkin's description of Orlando's relationships with Sasha and Euphrosyne, they note that these proclamations of "treachery" are also firmly gendered based on privilege. "Euphrosyne calls Orlando's actions treachery," they argue, "because he has followed passion rather than proscription," while "to Orlando, Sasha has betrayed his male privilege" (2002, 14). In allowing her audience to see Orlando as responsible for the end of both relationships, Potter wraps up the statements at hand ("the treachery of men" and "the treachery of women") simultaneously into Orlando. While we certainly do feel for Orlando in their naivety, earnestness, romantic aggression, and emotional growth, the film does not encourage us to harbour ill feelings for either Sasha or Euphrosyne. Instead, we have another early sign that both "male" and "female" romantic flaws are inherent to young Orlando.

This love triangle, much like Orlando's relationship with Queen Elizabeth, could be read in two key ways:

- as a heterosexual triangle between Euphrosyne (a woman), Sasha (a woman), and Orlando (a young man). Or,
- as a queer coupling between Euphrosyne (a woman), Sasha (a woman) and Tilda Swinton (a famous and frequently androgynous female actor).

In the case of this love triangle, even if we desire to read it as narratively heterosexual, it is futile to pretend that we can eliminate the queer implications. Every time an audience watches the film, a single fact is present: when Orlando kisses Sasha, we are watching two *women*. While individual viewers may find this moment to be queerly pleasurable or not, our suspension of disbelief breaks down in the moment of Orlando and Sasha's embrace. Potter has given us a uniquely queer moment: Tilda Swinton and Charlotte Valandrey engaged in a kiss.

NICK GREENE and THE KHAN

Throughout the film, Orlando repeatedly undergoes internal change and growth during periods of supernaturally long sleep, with their first transformational slumber occurring immediately after the end of their romance with

Figure 8
Orlando and Sasha (played by Charlotte Valandrey) kiss in this uniquely queer moment.

Sasha. The next era of the film, "1650," "POETRY," launches us into another key relationship in Orlando's development, one with the poet Nick Greene (played by Heathcote Williams) and, perhaps even more so, with the art of poetry itself. When we begin the "POETRY" chapter of Potter's film, Orlando is sitting alone in their library. High atop a ladder, they sit and read aloud from a condensed version of Shakespeare's "Sonnet 29": "When in disgrace with Fortune and men's eyes / I all alone beweepe my out-cast state, / And trouble heaven with my bootless cries / And look upon myself and curse my fate." "Ah, poetry," Orlando sighs longingly towards the camera.

Immediately after Orlando's solitary moment in the stacks of their library, we see Nick Greene approaching the doors of Orlando's estate. While I discuss Orlando's interaction with Greene in depth in the third chapter of this book, it is worth noting that, although the relationship with Greene is not romantic

Figure 9 Top
Nick Greene (played by Heathcote Williams) laps up soup while Orlando
opines about poetry.

Figure 10 Bottom
Orlando reads Shakespeare in their private library.

in the way that Orlando's relationship with Sasha is, Orlando and Greene's relationship does constitute a coupling in my eyes. In seeking out time with Greene, Orlando's continual search for "company" places this relationship in league with the other couplings throughout the film. At the moment Greene arrives, Orlando is giddy to meet him. Orlando, who we have seen writing and reciting poetry since the first moments of the film, is clearly trying to woo a fickle Greene. Greene, on the other hand, is only willing to spend time reading and critiquing Orlando's poetry if Orlando is willing to become his patron – granting Greene a yearly allowance, paid quarterly. Orlando, eager to win Greene's affections (and mind, perhaps), agrees.

While their relationship constitutes a patronage and not a romance in the context of the film, we might read the moments shared by Orlando and Greene in queerly inflected ways. In their obvious affection for Greene – or at least of Greene's body (of work) – Orlando ultimately weds themself to him by agreeing to pay his pension in hopes that love (for Orlando's work) may be reciprocated. What transpires, however, is far from affection, looking more like a loveless marriage. Upon his departure from Orlando's estate, Greene pens a scathing critique of Orlando's poetry, sent to them in a letter that functions like an emotional divorce. Reading the letter in front of a bonfire, Orlando is filled with rage. After reading, they ask their valet to "drop this [letter] in the midst of the filthiest manure." Nevertheless, Orlando agrees to continue to pay Greene's pension – Orlando is wedded to Greene and will continue to hold up their end of the bargain.

After Greene rebukes their affection, Orlando looks straight into the camera once again. Orlando is visibly broken and angry, their red hair accentuated by the green of the grass and orange of the fire burning behind them. Although they stay silent in this moment, Orlando might as well be saying, "the treachery of poets." With their gaze directed straight into the camera's lens, it is a moment that mirrors Orlando's glare into the camera after Sasha has abandoned them. This similarity in tone reinforces the understanding that Greene's re-

Figure 11
The Khan (played by Lothaire Bluteau) greets Orlando upon their arrival in Khiva.

buke is just as painful for Orlando as Sasha's was – these relationships have more in common than first meets the eye.

Orlando's misery after Greene's rejection leads them to take a wildly different path, asking the King if they can become an ambassador. Obliging, the King sends Orlando "East" to Khiva, Uzbekistan, where it's clear that Orlando is being sent on a colonization effort. As the music swells, signalling another change in Orlando's life, we are greeted with title cards that read "1700," "POLITICS." Now more than one hundred years old and looking just as young as ever (the biggest change in their appearance being the newly fashionable long wig), Orlando has divorced themselves from England.

Upon their arrival in Khiva, Orlando is greeted by the Khan (played by Lothaire Bluteau), who invites Orlando to call upon him for "any of his needs." The placid tone of their conversation quickly shifts as the Khan airs concern as to Orlando's presence in his domain. In the Khan's words, "the English have a habit of collecting countries." Orlando, seemingly unaware (or continually naive) of the implications of their own presence, responds that England has "no designs on your sovereignty at all." The Khan responds by asking, "you would assist us in defence against mutual enemies?" Orlando, unsure how to respond, says nothing at all, looking blankly at the Khan.

For Orlando, on a multicentury quest for love and companionship, the concept of physical violence is unfathomable. The perpetually young Orlando has, at this point in their life, been given every material comfort. They have a rich library all their own, they have valets and servants, they have an estate, they have (in the words of Nick Greene's scathing critique) "dogs, dogs, more dogs and far too many rooms," and – in their new interaction with the Khan – they have elected to travel "east." And while companionship has continually eluded them, material goods have not. It is from this privileged standpoint that Orlando's blank gaze to the Khan is telling: theirs is a privilege of leisure as well as property. A request for them to personally take up arms becomes a crisis of masculine identity partly because of this privilege. In the scene that follows, the Khan and Orlando sit together in the desert in what functions, effectively, as a drinking contest. Drunk, Orlando wraps their arm around the Khan (he is, after all, company), toasting to "the manly virtues." Amongst these, Orlando is able to name only "loyalty" and "courage," pausing but failing to think of more. Here, Orlando forgets stereotypical associations with masculine "strength," instead focusing on the interpersonal traits that they hold in such high regard despite seeing their own relationships repeatedly erode. Once again, while the film's audience is made to empathize with Orlando, we are not immune to seeing and cringing at their naivety.

Orlando is clearly feeling at home and calm in this new land. Listening to a group of "traveling musicians" (Potter and Woolf 1994, 34) at a party after their drinks with the Khan, Orlando removes their peruke,[8] signalling a shift in their comfortability and a split from their lingering ties to England. The film then cuts to a shot of Orlando relaxing alone in a hammam, dressed in

Figure 12 Top
Orlando and the Khan toast the "manly virtues."

Figure 13 Bottom
Orlando relaxes in a *tableau vivant*.

a simple robe and turban, taking in the heat and light that fills the room. We spend an extended moment alone with Orlando, gazing at them as they throw their head back in what feels like a beautifully composed *tableau vivant*. We are then greeted with an interruption: a distinctly British voice aggressively proclaims, "Take me to your master … I said take me to your master. Does he speak English?" Barging into the room, we see the Archduke Harry (played by John Wood) dressed in full military regalia. Harry is stunned at Orlando's appearance – something between horror and nervous lust manifests on Harry's trembling lips. Although it is unclear how much time has passed from Orlando's arrival in Khiva to this moment in the sauna, Harry informs us that "Her Majesty" would like to celebrate Orlando's "ten years here as ambassador" by "raising [Orlando] to the highest rank in the peerage." Clearly wishing that the Archduke had not come, Orlando simply replies "ah." This is a marked turn for Orlando who, at every other moment in the film, has welcomed companionship, although it has always been on their terms.

The Archduke insists on a party for Orlando, at which they will receive their commendation. When that party comes, however, no guests arrive. The Archduke moves to begin the ceremony with only his own travelling companions present but, just as the Archduke begins, Orlando is whisked away by two palace guards. What transpires is, to my mind, one of the most queerly inflected moments of the film: as the guards usher Orlando to speak with the Khan, an emotionally hurt Orlando says, "I was expecting you as a guest at my party, I didn't realize you were entertaining hostilities." The Khan, shot in a beautiful, soft close-up with the light of a fire bouncing off of his cheeks, looks to Orlando with all the hurt of a scorned lover. The Khan responds, "I was warned that Englishmen would be dangerous for me. But I would like to give you an opportunity to prove this wrong." The Archduke rushes into frame in a medium two shot, standing next to Orlando with a flurry of nervous energy. "Let me introduce you," says Orlando, "this is the Archduke Harry from England." Both the Archduke and the Khan's eyes move back and forth from

Orlando to one another. We have clearly entered another love triangle, but this time both the Archduke and the Khan are vying for Orlando's affection.[9]

"Orlando," the Khan says, "our enemies are at the city wall. Will you help?" "You wish me to take arms?" asks Orlando. "Surely, Orlando, you, an English*man*, are not afraid" (emphasis mine), responds the Khan. Orlando is forced to make a decision: the threat of violence, that "strength" that remained unspoken in Orlando's toast ten years prior, has come to a testing point. Although they are visibly displeased, Orlando agrees to distribute arms. Moving towards the Khan, they are once again positioned in front of a bonfire, echoing the moment at which Orlando's relationship with Nick Greene dissolved. Throughout the film, bonfires represent an internal rage in Orlando that manifests when they see their most prized relationships slipping through their grasp.

Although this scene becomes a show of "masculine virtue" with the Khan asking Orlando to engage in acts of violence, the queer implications are palpable. A catalyst for the dissolution of Orlando's relationship with the Khan, the Archduke functions as a surprise third wheel in what appears to have been an uninterrupted ten-year romance. With the three men standing together, Orlando and the Khan both read as scorned lovers. The Khan feels betrayed by the British (and thereby Orlando), while Orlando is hurt by being forced to choose between maintaining a relationship they cherish (with the Khan) and maintaining their value of love over violence.

As Orlando, the Khan, and the Archduke all rush to the city wall, Orlando and the Khan embrace while explosions flash around them. Orlando's presence, here, is a show of love for the Khan, but at what price? Handed a gun by the Archduke, Orlando is clearly baffled. While Orlando inspects the weapon (this may very well be the first moment Orlando has held a firearm), the Archduke sees and shoots an intruder who has made it over the top of the wall. Orlando rushes to the shot man, inspecting his wounds, but the Archduke instructs Orlando to "leave him." With empathy, Orlando responds that "this is a dying man." The Archduke corrects Orlando nonchalantly: "he's not a man; he's the enemy." This dehumanizing remark is too much for Orlando, who looks straight into the camera again, highlighting Orlando's ideological break with this culture of violence and "masculine virtue." Literally walking away from the fight in the next shot, it is clear that if this is what it means to be a "man," Orlando is not interested.

Back in bed after another seven-day, transformational slumber, we see Orlando's stunning body blending beautifully with the bedding that envelops them. Removing their blonde peruke against the eggshell sheets, Orlando's hair is a vibrant red – now nearly as long as their wig. Dust fills the air as we cut to a close-up of a shimmering bath. Orlando dips their hands into the water, splashing it against their face. With dust particles glittering on screen, Orlando turns towards an ornate mirror, exposing their nude and distinctly female body. While Orlando gazes at themself in the mirror, a slight smile greets their lips. "Same person," Orlando says to themself, "no difference at all." Turning to the camera, Orlando speaks directly to us: "just a different sex." Ultimately, Orlando's relationship with the Khan – and subsequent realization that "manliness" is fundamentally tied to "violence" – triggers their shift to a "different sex." The glitter bath that cleanses Orlando of their masculine baggage signals a shift in Orlando's gendered understanding of themself but, as Orlando makes clear, this change does not signal a radical transformation in their larger sense of self.

THE ARCHDUKE HARRY and SHELMERDINE

Making their way back to their estate after their awakening, Orlando approaches their door in an ominous black robe. Walking away from the camera in wide shot, Orlando's body becomes a black void against a vivid image of their childhood home. Orlando greets their housekeeper and butler with a simple, "well, here I am again," leaving the two servants perplexed. Who is this figure wrapped in black robes? This is certainly not the male ambassador for whom they were waiting. Our next shot is a close-up of Orlando's torso, now adorned in a white corset, which is being laced by one of Orlando's servants. Walking down to a long gallery, with furniture draped in white cloth, Orlando attempts to manoeuvre with an "enormously wide crinoline" (Potter and Woolf 1994, 42). In this moment, Suzanne Ferriss and Kathleen Waites's argument that *Orlando* uses the "unreliable signifiers of fashion for gender and gender for identity" in order to "expos[e] and subver[t]" is palpable. While heteronormative dress may encourage us to understand the relationship between fashion and gender as linked cleanly and fundamentally, this moment in *Orlando* forces us to acknowledge how artificial those connections are. The monochromatic colour shift from simple black to elaborate white garment is striking, as is our first image of Orlando adorned as a woman. In wardrobe designer Sandy Powell's hands, Orlando is simultaneously stunning and absurd, oscillating between embodying death and re-birth.[10]

Two title cards read "1750," "society." Entering a party given by a woman known for her "literary gatherings," we are greeted by a beautiful rococo mise-en-scene. Extravagant pink gowns and yellow frocks adorn the bodies of those attending the gathering, with their outfits contrasted against the large black and white checkered floor. Everything about this scene's mise-en-scene – and the mechanical way in which characters exist within the world of the salon that Potter has created – screams artifice. As the camera pans, we see that the Archduke Harry is seated in a corner of the room with a small group. Harry, in an obvious split from his fellow guests, argues that he finds "science to be more interesting than poetry." His face, grinning widely, makes plain his naivety. Attempting to rationalize his comment to the group, Harry is caught off guard when Orlando, adorned in an absurdly elaborate teal gown, "exaggerated clothing and immensely high wig," enters the room. As Orlando sits, their crinoline makes their hips so wide that they take up a sofa fit for three.

Figure 14
Orlando navigates the halls of their home in an enormous crinoline.

Fumbling with a fan and "confused about what is expected of her" (Potter and Woolf 1994, 45), Orlando sits alone. The Archduke is visibly awestruck by their appearance.

Ushered towards the conversation with Mr Pope, Mr Addison, and Mr Swift, Orlando is given the chance to sit with real-life literary figures.[11] Misogynistic and self-important, the three poets state that they "consider woman as a beautiful, romantic animal who should be adorned in furs and feathers, pearls and diamonds … every woman is at best a contradiction. And frankly, most women have no characters at all." Fuming, Orlando responds that they "find it strange" that these men are "poets … [who] speak of [their] muse in the feminine, and yet you appear to feel neither tenderness nor respect towards

Figure 15
Orlando in an absurdly elaborate teal gown.

your wives nor towards females in general." In this interaction, Ferriss and Waites argue, "clothing ... does more than simply mark femininity (or masculinity); among the poets, at least, it conditions their responses" (1999, 112). Critics of Potter's film argue that she moves away from feminist thought, in favour of a "postfeminist world of gender equality" (Hollinger and Winterhalter 2001, 250), but Orlando's words to their literary audience read to me as far more aggressively feminist than some scholars are willing to acknowledge. Ferriss and Waites rightfully argue that Orlando's "apt critique on the incongruity between [the poets'] esteem for a female muse and lack of regard for females generally is rendered mute by the testimony of her dress" (1999, 112). However, I also see Orlando's anger towards these men and, thereby, towards a misogynistic history of masculinist values in art making as providing voice to the argument that there is a longstanding (and continuing) "oppression via gender" (Hollinger and Winterhalter 2001, 249),[12] an oppression of which Orlando is only beginning to recognize the extent.

Rushing from this encounter, the Archduke trails Orlando, who is now also being pursued by two government officials. These officials inform Orlando that Orlando is now party to "several major lawsuits" concerning their ownership over their family home due to their change in sex – despite having been given the estate by Queen Elizabeth I directly in 1592. Taking this opportunity to court Orlando, the Archduke turns, grasping Orlando's arm and offering them his hand in marriage. When Orlando claims that they "don't quite understand," the Archduke confesses that "to me, you were and always will be, whether male or female, the pink, the pearl, and the perfection of your sex." At this line, Potter cuts to a shot of the two officials, who look horrified. Although Orlando and the Archduke met while Orlando was understood as a "man," the Archduke does not romantically pursue Orlando until they are understood as a "woman." A seemingly heterosexual encounter on the surface, the Archduke's advance is also queer precisely because he positions his lust for Orlando as having existed prior to their identification as "female." Laughing in response to the Archduke's proposal, Orlando replies "Oh! Archduke!

That's so very kind of you, yes. I cannot accept." The Archduke responds that "I am England and you are mine" because "I adore you," a response that mirrors Orlando's to Sasha earlier in the film. Highlighting the fluid nature of Orlando's being, the Archduke attempts to pressure Orlando into accepting his offer by saying that "with your ambiguous sexuality, which I am prepared to tolerate, this is your last chance of respectability." But the joke is on the Archduke, here: his ability to "tolerate" Orlando's "ambiguous sexuality" reads instead as a thirst for Orlando's "ambiguous" embodiment.

This proposal scene is also crucial to an understanding of the film as queer in relationship to time. In the Archduke's pronouncement that they have *always* found Orlando attractive, we are invited to think back to the prior incarnation of their relationship, while Orlando was a man in Khiva. If Orlando's relationship with the Archduke was leading towards this surface level heterosexually all along, are we to understand this now-female Orlando to have been the same person in relationships with Queen Elizabeth, Sasha, and Euphrosyne? If we understand Tilda Swinton's body to have remained static (and perpetually female) throughout the film, the Archduke's revelation concretizes the sense that was hinted at earlier: that Orlando's former relationships were queer as well.

Although the Archduke may desire ambiguity, Orlando's next relationship – with an American explorer named Shelmerdine (played by Billy Zane) – pairs ambiguity with ambiguity. We find Shelmerdine in a new era of the film, "1850," "SEX." Orlando has just fled the scene with the Archduke, transforming from "her pale decorated eighteenth-century clothes and wig, to a dark-green Victorian jacket and crinoline" (Potter and Woolf 1994, 49). In Woolf's *Orlando* (discussed in more depth in the following chapter of this book), Shelmerdine is described as like a woman – Orlando cries, playfully, "you're a woman, Shel!" And Shelmerdine responds, "you're a man, Orlando!" In these interactions in Woolf's novel, their relationship is clearly and directly about the ambiguity of gender or, as theorist George Piggford has argued, about "radically disconnecting sex and gender" (1997, 53). While there is less gender

Figure 16
Shelmerdine (played by Billy Zane) gazes off-screen at Orlando.

play in their relationship in Potter's film, we still see an inversion of normatively gendered relationships.

When they first meet, Shelmerdine falls off his horse, twists his ankle, and
is in need of care from Orlando. Simultaneously a damsel in distress and the
single most conventionally masculine character in the film, Shelmerdine is a
"dark-haired, wild-looking and extremely handsome" man in Potter's film
(Potter and Woolf 1994, 51). Lying on the ground, Orlando and Shelmerdine
look into each other's eyes – it is Shelmerdine who has the wild mane of hair,
contrasted against Orlando's well put-together Victorian ensemble. Immediately after meeting, Orlando asks Shelmerdine if he will marry them, to which
he playfully responds, "ma'am, I would gladly. But I fear my ankle is twisted."

Figure 17 Top
Potter imagines the transformation from "pale decorated eighteenth-century clothes and wig, to a dark-green Victorian jacket and crinoline" in the maze at Hatfield House.

Figure 18 Bottom
Orlando runs through the maze at Hatfield House.

Back at Orlando's estate after a night of assumed lovemaking, we see Orlando and Shelmerdine lying naked in bed. "Orlando lies above Shelmerdine and caresses him tentatively and joyfully" while "Shelmerdine remains resolutely passive" (Potter and Woolf 1994, 54). Orlando is framed in a high angle shot, looking directly into the camera. This framing and positioning is strikingly masculine, with Shelmerdine lying curled around Orlando, who is clearly in control of the situation. Even in this romantic coupling, where the film clearly establishes Orlando as "woman" and Shelmerdine as "man," Orlando's gaze disrupts our understanding of the gendered conventions of their relationship.

With the film split into discrete periods in which Orlando is understood as a "man" and then as a "woman," we are invited to think transhistorically. As an audience, the film invites us to ask: what does it mean for the heterosexuality of these romantic couplings that Orlando has been in relationships with women when they are a "man" but then with men when they are "woman"? If we are to understand Orlando as the "same person, just a different sex," how are we to understand their past, present, and future relationships in either hetero- or homosexual terms? These questions are central to an interpretation of *Orlando* that sees the film as an example of LGBT representation; perhaps Orlando is bisexual, desiring relationships with both men and women. But the film provides us roadblocks to that reading: why *are* Orlando's romantic partners so clearly demarcated by their own socially perceived sex? The fact that the film leaves this question so murky, that Potter assures us that Orlando is the "same person ... just a different sex," and that the film engages so clearly with questions about the performance of gender points to the film's more radically queer potential. Through an exploration of these questions, it becomes apparent that the film is much more invested in a diffusion of identity than its heterosexual pairings first seem to suggest.

Figure 19 Top
Orlando and Shelmerdine lie in the grass during their first meeting.

Figure 20 Bottom
Orlando looks straight into the camera while Shelmerdine curls around them.

THE PEASANT and THE KING

I want to end this close reading of the film by focusing on one last relationship that holds implications for how we might understand Potter's engagement with and adaptation of Woolf's text (which is the core concern of the following chapter). Although not a coupling per se, Potter's "1610" ("LOVE") chapter begins with one of the most striking images in the film: just before we meet Princess Sasha, we see King James I (played by Dudley Sutton) and his valets standing in a field of snow, staring into the ice below them. The film launches us from the summer of Orlando's youth into what Woolf describes as "The Great Frost," where "birds froze in mid-air" and "a young countrywoman started to cross the road in her usual robust health and was seen by the on-lookers to turn visibly to powder" (Woolf [1928] 2006, 33). "But while the country people suffered the extremity of want," Woolf writes, "London en-joyed a carnival of the utmost brilliancy" ([1928] 2006, 34). In this flurry of ice and cold, Woolf describes a striking divide between the classes – the wealthy living well, literally playing on top of the frozen corpses of "eels" and an "old bumboat woman," who had frozen mid-apple delivery. In Potter's *Orlando*, this is what we see: from King James's point of view, we are greeted with a figure suspended below King James's feet in the ice, a peasant locked in suspended animation, with apples scattered in space and frozen in time around her. In Woolf's words, ".twas a sight King James specially liked to look upon ... nothing could exceed the brilliancy and gaiety of the scene by day" ([1928] 2006, 36). In Woolf as in Potter, the relationship between King James and the woman in the ice is one of hierarchy drenched in class critique – the King is positioned literally on top of the woman in space, but he is also metaphorically "above" her in terms of wealth and status. His joviality is de-pendent upon her suffering and loss. While the relationship is not romantic, it is clearly one that indicts the British class system.

The Great Frost, like many details in Woolf's *Orlando*, was a historical event in Britain during the winter of 1607–08. As Caroline Davies explains in the

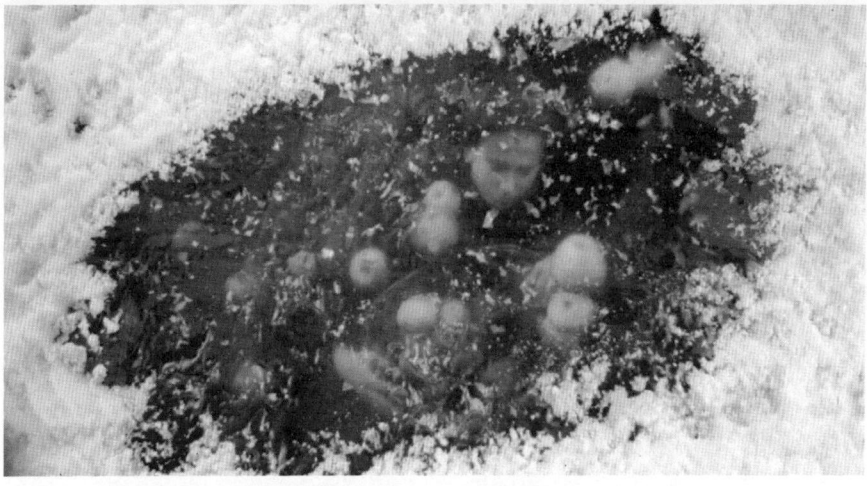

Figure 21 Top
King James I (played by Dudley Sutton) and his valets standing in a field of snow, staring into the ice below them.

Figure 22 Bottom
A peasant is locked in suspended animation, with apples scattered in space and frozen in time around her.

Guardian, "between 1309 and 1814, during which Britain was said to have experienced a 'little ice age,' the Thames froze at least 23 times, and on five of those occasions impromptu frost fairs – described as being a cross between a Christmas market, circus and boisterous party – were held. At the time of the first frost fair, in 1608, the river froze over for six weeks" (2021). While both Woolf and Potter highlight the strange joviality that Davies describes above, their critiques of class are different with regard to issues of time.

In Woolf's hands, the Frost serves as a narrative device by which she is able to indict the upper classes, making royalty grotesque by allowing them the opportunity to literally dance on the (icy) graves of the poor who have become trapped below. In Potter's cinematic adaptation, that contempt for King James I (and the complex system of oppression he represents) is maintained, but Potter uses the moving image medium to add on an additional layer of embodied critique. Where Woolf describes the body frozen in ice as an "old bumboat woman," Potter's peasant is locked in her youth, much like Orlando will be for the entirety of the film. This perpetual youth is a clear break from what critical theorist Elizabeth Freeman has described as "chrononormativity," a process by which "naked flesh is bound into socially meaningful embodiment through temporal regulation" which uses "time to organize individual human bodies toward maximum productivity" (2010, 3) in our everyday experience of being in the world.

Thinking about the frozen woman's trajectory within a conventional, linear, capitalist logic, one can assume that, at some point, the ice will thaw and this (probably) dead woman's body will rush forth. The apples will melt and might either be swept away or eaten; her body will decay; there will be some productive return to chrononormativity from which this weather event has provided a momentary break. This return to normalcy is an explicit and graphic detail in Woolf's *Orlando* that was present in earlier drafts of Potter's script, only to be underplayed in Potter's finished film. In Woolf's text, the Thames thaws in front of Orlando's eyes, gushing "turbulent yellow waters" at sunrise. "But what was the most awful and inspiring of terror," writes Woolf at length, "was the sight of the human creatures who had been trapped in the night and now paced their twisting and precarious islands in the utmost agony of spirit" ([1928] 2006, 62). At the moment in which Sasha betrays Orlando in Woolf's text, the natural world punishes those who have been jovial in the space of others' misfortune, simultaneously returning the reader to what Freeman has described as the "common sense" of temporal existence in the "present tense" (2010, xv).

While Potter's film does continue past the winter of 1609 and while we do see the ice crack during a subjective moment in which Orlando escapes their feelings for Sasha, we never see peasants turn to powder nor do we see bodies floating in or being extracted from the river. In Woolf's novel, it is these moments that provide the grotesque evidence of the peasants' death. Instead, in Potter's film, we only see two helpless people drift by in a sea of ice. The impact is simply not the same. Because we never see a grand moment of thaw as we do in Woolf's novel, Potter leaves her peasant woman in a state of frozen time, neither "alive" in a conventional sense nor deceased. While we may know, in our rational minds, that she is likely dead beneath the ice, our experience as filmgoers with an awareness of supernatural cinematic grammar complicates any simple read of this moment. After all, in other cinematic works of fantasy, individuals *do*, in fact, come back to life from moments of frozen stasis.

The potentiality of this frozen woman's existence is never fully foreclosed by a clear, descriptive death as is the case in Woolf's moment of thaw. Instead, she teeters in a space between life and death – imbued with possibility created by the trauma from which it springs. This level of potentiality that manifests through trauma is in accord with Freeman's idea that "queer becoming-collective-across-time and even the concept of futurity itself are predicated upon injury … or trauma that precede and determine bodiliness itself" (2010, 11). To this extent, I understand the frozen woman's unconventional relationship to time beneath the ice to constitute a "queer time" insofar as it "counter[s] the common sense of the present tense" (xv)[13] without fully foreclosing her future potential.

In this brief scene, we are presented with two distinct relationships to temporal existence, with the ice functioning as a finite divider. Above the ice, time continues along normatively. Below the ice, chrononormativity is eschewed. Where Woolf's text allows us a moment of catharsis (nature always wins) that ultimately returns us to a singular and familiar flow of time, Potter's film does not. Through this omission, the systems of power (with which Orlando is complicit) are implicated in the intersectional relationship between capital, class, gender, embodiment, and time, all of which can and historically have been regulated to manifest capitalist gain (from which Orlando has benefitted).

The frozen woman's break from chrononormativity also allows us an avenue by which to think about the overarching queerness of cinematic time. In not releasing the frozen peasant from her stasis, Potter keeps her locked behind a cold, transparent screen of ice. This allows the young, apple-wielding woman to embody the Queen's request to Orlando – this woman "[will] not fade. [Will] not wither. [Will] not grow old." Potter's ice-woman is trapped behind a glassy screen and, through editing and the construction of the film, *she* is able to remain in perpetual youth. King James's screen of ice mirrors our own cinematic frame of Orlando. This fleeting shot of the peasant's body locked in agelessness under the ice, then, becomes an allegory for the way that cinema allows us to relentlessly capture youth, linking Freeman's "queer time" with film theorist André Bazin's argument that cinema provides unparalleled (and beyond human) access to time (as articulated in his 1949 essay "Death Every Afternoon").

In what we might understand to be cinema's uniquely queer relationship to temporality, Bazin writes that while "I cannot repeat a single moment of my life … cinema can repeat any one of these moments indefinitely before my eyes" (30). By definition, images become fixed and repeatable in time on film. Orlando will not grow old because Swinton's cinematic body cannot age; every body on every screen is captured in a state of perpetual suspended animation, fated to live out a fixed film in eternal, repeatable, and potentially endless temporal arrangement. The act of narrative filmmaking is a violence all its own that invites both viewer and subject to engage queerly with time; beautiful, yes, but a way of creating a superhuman stasis without a thaw. Potter's film reminds us that cinematic time is an inherently queer version of our own temporal reality.

Chapter 2
the politics of a daughter
(adaptation and the making of *Orlando*)

Interviews and reviews from the release of Sally Potter's *Orlando* repeatedly highlight the fact that the film was the culmination of a monumental, years-long collaboration between Potter and her crew. In a 2019 special issue of *Aperture* magazine, Potter explains that "by the spring of 1988 [five years before the release of *Orlando*], years of trying to convince financiers that *Orlando* was a makeable film had led nowhere" (Potter 2019, 34). Potter had been told repeatedly that *Orlando* was "unadaptable because of its massive scope ... its central conceit, and Woolf's playful and ironic style of narration, which depends upon written language for its effect" (Fowler 2009, 61).

One of Potter's key developments towards seeing *Orlando* realized was the casting of Tilda Swinton in the titular role. Recounting her involvement in the film, Tilda Swinton describes her first encounter with Sally Potter as fortuitous, with their relationship quickly becoming collaborative (West and West 1993, 18). Potter had come to see Swinton in a performance of the play *Man to Man* (which ran at London's Royal Court Theatre in 1988). Having read Woolf's novel when she was fifteen, Swinton explains that *Orlando* "seemed to provide for me another angle at which to come at the problem of gender specification, which was not to examine an occluded gender ... but an idea of limitlessness through the concept of immortality." After Potter attended *Man to Man*, she and Swinton began talking about adapting Woolf's novel. "At the very beginning," Swinton explains "for about eighteen months,

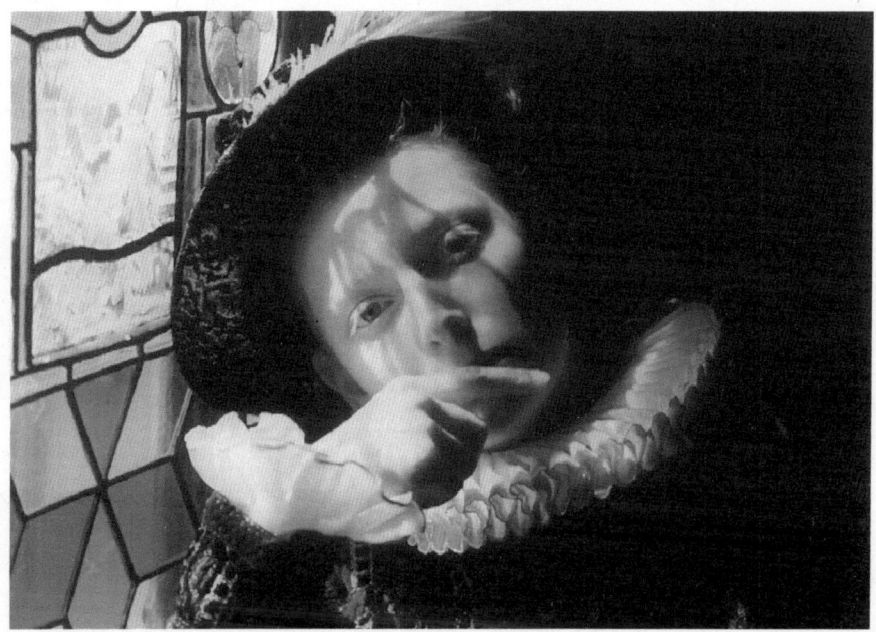

Figure 23
Swinton poses as the male Orlando at Vita Sackville-West's childhood home, Knole.

it was just the two of us, the idea, and the book. There was no script, no money, and no producer" (West and West 1993, 18). Having Swinton signed on to the project, Potter had an idea to get things started: "what if I were to take some photographs that looked as though the film had already been made? … Tilda was game, as she always was. We hired some costumes and set off … to Knole, the fourteenth century estate on which Vita Sackville-West grew up. She changed, and we stepped swiftly over the velvet ropes behind which one was supposed to just stand and admire" (Potter 2019, 34). Potter crafted one hundred copies of a book, xeroxed and glued by hand, that provided potential investors and executives a visual sense that this film

Figure 24
Swinton poses as the female Orlando at Vita Sackville-West's childhood
home, Knole.

could, in fact, be made. The photographs, while not solidifying financial support for the film, are stunning both as works of art and as a crucial element of Potter's development process. The twenty-three photographs provide the first visual glimpses into the world that Potter was conceptualizing, inserting her imagining of Orlando (as embodied by Swinton) into the historical world of Woolf's text (Sackville-West's Knole).

As years passed and the film remained in developmental limbo, the production team was forced to radically cut down the film's budget, which was originally estimated to cost between $30 million (Potter 2019, 34) and $40 million (*Washington Post* 1993). By the time Potter and her team moved closer to production, the budget for the film had been reduced to $10.6 million. Just before shooting, the budget needed to be reduced again to $3.8 million (Fowler 2009, 59). It took Potter and the film's producer, Christopher Sheppard, about nine years to see *Orlando* through from development to completion,[1] with Potter and Sheppard ultimately needing to remortgage their houses to pay for expenses in development that were not covered by funders (Fowler 2009, 59). Despite all of these challenges, "Christopher Sheppard somehow, in 1991, pulled together a five-country coproduction, and we made the film for $4 million, shooting on the frozen sea in the Gulf of Finland in Saint Petersburg, in the desert in Uzbekistan, and in the halls and on the grounds of Hatfield House" (Potter 2019, 34).[2] When the film wrapped, Potter's crew had shot *Orlando* for roughly 10 per cent of the initial estimated budget.

For many news sources covering the film upon its release, the film's visuals were only made more impressive by these developmental and preproduction challenges. Early reviews for the film, which celebrate its stunning cinematography, costumes, and desert and ice scenes, are also eager to provide narratives of its harrowing production. In one example, the Washington Post's glowing review revels in the fact that "on location in Uzbekistan, the crew couldn't afford a hotel, so they stayed in a converted mosque that ran water for only a few hours a day" (*Washington Post* 1993). *Orlando* is a visual achievement by any standard, but the way it was produced only added to the critical astonishment.

Celebrating the film's achievement as an adaptation, Richard Corliss wrote in *Time* magazine that "anyone – man or woman or a new, improved species – could have made *Orlando*. But until Sally Potter, nobody did. Nobody dared" (Corliss and Welch 1993). This common thread – that the film should be considered as a brave work of adaptation – proliferated from the moment of the film's release; articles frequently revel in the split between the assumed "unadaptability" of Woolf's text and Potter's beautiful onscreen display. Film scholars have also been fascinated with the issues of adaptation that surround

Figure 25
Sally Potter and producer Christopher Sheppard on the set of *Orlando*.

the shift from novel to film, with many focusing specifically on questions of "authorship" that arise when a germinal text is adapted.[3] This has been the case, in large part, because Potter framed her project as a "translation rather than an adaptation" (Reviron-Piégay 2009, 317), often making "ruthless" changes where needed to visualize the novel for the screen (Potter and Woolf 1994, ix). Adaptation theorist Floriane Reviron-Piégay, for example, notes the ways in which scholars hold cinematic adaptations to impossible standards of fidelity while also faulting Potter's film for its breaks from Woolf's novel in content and style (2009). Film scholar So Mayer, who has published extensively on Potter's films, has worked to counter these lines of criticism, providing unique, nuanced arguments for how we might understand Potter's modifications to Woolf's text. Whether celebrating or criticizing Potter's work, choices made during the adaptation process remain a key element of the way that scholars have understood the film.

Given that many scholars have understood the film as – first and foremost – an adapted work, an in-depth analysis of Potter's screenplay drafts provides necessary context that is lacking from much of the literature about Potter's *Orlando*. This avenue of research has become possible thanks in large part to Potter's own archive of production documents and screenplay drafts, which her company made available online starting in 2008 via a site called SP-ARK (the Sally Potter Archive). In the four years that *Orlando* was in development, Sally Potter wrote somewhere between twelve (*Washington Post* 1993) and forty (Mayer 2009, 91) drafts of the script, four of which are clearly demarcated and available on SP-ARK. These drafts include:

1 A handwritten draft completed in 1988. This was the same year that Potter and Tilda Swinton began collaborating together, producing their first "presentation book" for the film. This presentation book pitched the film to potential investors and featured photographs of Swinton as Orlando.
2 A typewritten draft completed in 1989.
3 A typewritten draft completed in 1990. This was the same year that Potter produced a second presentation book to aid in a series of meetings she took for the film at the Cannes Film Festival.
4 A typewritten draft completed in 1991, the year before production began on *Orlando*.

Collectively, these drafts illuminate Potter's own description of her adaptation process, which she describes in her "Notes on the Adaptation of the Book *Orlando*" as "find[ing] a way of remaining true to the spirit of the book and to Virginia Woolf's intentions, whilst being ruthless with changing the book in any way necessary to make it work cinematically … The most immediate changes were structural. The storyline was simplified – any events which did not significantly further Orlando's story were dropped. The narrative also needed to be *driven*. Whereas the novel could withstand abstraction and arbitrariness (such as Orlando's change of sex) cinema is more pragmatic. There had to be reasons – however flimsy – to propel us along a journey based itself on a kind of suspension of disbelief" (Sony Pictures Classics, emphasis in original). In this description, Potter highlights two competing impulses: first, to distill and make the film centrally about Orlando's character, and second, to explain and provide cause for the film's narrative events. Looking at the four drafts mentioned above in a chronological fashion, this chapter will track changes in Potter's adaptation of Woolf's novel, working through *Orlando*'s morphing relationship with queerness while keeping the so-called "unadaptable" nature of this specific text in frame.

It would be impossible to chart all of the changes from draft to draft, and such an approach would make for a truly monotonous read. Instead, I want to use this chapter as a space to point to some of the central changes, especially those that might help us understand how the film grapples with sex and sexuality. This is a project that So Mayer has begun in productive ways, both in their journal article ("The Mirror Didn't Crack" from 2008) and in their monograph about Potter's oeuvre (*A Politics of Love* from 2009). Mayer was an early part of SP-ARK, serving as the archive's educational consultant and their writing draws upon many of the archive's resources. While Mayer notes specific changes between drafts of *Orlando* in their discussions of the film, their descriptions of these draft-level changes are brief. Acknowledging the way in which Mayer's writing has laid the groundwork for my analysis, this chapter elaborates on draft-level changes in depth. In so doing, I trace the development of Sally Potter's *Orlando* from a relatively faithful adaptation of Woolf's novel (with overt lesbian relationships) to one rich with queer "question marks," whose voice is made possible by the "ruthless" changes from the page to the screen.

To accomplish this, I have structured this chapter around the four drafts accessible via SP-ARK, often considering them alongside the published screenplay for the film (published by Faber and Faber in 1994). This published version of the screenplay is particularly helpful for thinking about the way that Potter was conceptualizing the non-verbal moments on screen during and after the film's production by way of screen direction and description. In moving through these documents in this chapter, I pay particular attention to the way the framing of Orlando's key relationships changes between drafts. Of specific interest for charting Potter's shift from faithful adaptation to radical reimagining are Orlando's relationships with: Queen Elizabeth I (played by Quentin Crisp in the finished film, whose role shifted dramatically between screenplay drafts); the Archduke Harry (played by John Wood in the finished film, who, in early drafts, played a much larger role throughout the film as the Archduchess Harriett, a version of the Archduke in drag); Nell (a prostitute that Orlando hires as a woman, present in varying capacity in early drafts of the film but eliminated entirely in the finished film); and Orlando's child (who is a boy in Woolf's novel, is missing entirely from Potter's early screenplay drafts, and then is conceptualized as a daughter in Potter's finished film).

By focusing on these characters across drafts, this chapter draws methodologically from the work of adaptation theorists Julie Sanders and Pamela Demory. Sanders's *Adaptation and Appropriation* provides a framework for thinking through the "pleasure" that "exists, and persists, then, in the act of reading in, around, and on (and on)." Sanders argues that "it is the very endurance and survival of the source text that enables the ongoing process of juxtaposed readings that are crucial to the cultural operations of adaptation, and the ongoing experiences of pleasure for the reader or spectator in tracing the intertextual relationships" (2006, 25). For Demory, "a queer adaptation (and adaptation that queers) has the potential to disrupt and disorient heteronormative narrative and stylistic conventions" (2019, 9). For Demory, by its very nature, adaptation is always already queer. I use these theorists' work, taken together, as a methodological entry point to think about the way that

Potter's *Orlando* evolved queerly through drafts, taking pleasure in the charting of those changes.[4]

DRAFT ONE: adaptation as faithful translation

Potter's first, handwritten draft of *Orlando* (labelled "10/11/1988") is far more faithful to the plot points of Woolf's novel than the published screenplay. In this draft, we see Potter attempting to bring the novel, nearly verbatim, into the screenplay format. Thus, many of the central relationships – with Queen Elizabeth, the Archduke, and Nell, for example – appear in almost identical form to those in Woolf's novel.

In the finished film, the Queen quickly and obviously comes to adore Orlando. After their first meeting in the banquet hall, we see the two of them "walking in the grounds of the house, with dogs trotting beside them." There is affection and it is clear that the Queen enjoys Orlando's company, but Orlando's presence in these moments is more in line with the dogs – trotting alongside the Queen – than as a romantic interest. During Orlando and the Queen's time together, we learn that Orlando's family does not own the estate on which they reside; their home is a piece of property owned by the Queen. By the end of Orlando's encounter with the Queen, she has turned over the deed to the property on one condition: that Orlando never age. This serves as a commandment, sending Orlando (who presumably *has* aged up through this point in their youth) into perpetual agelessness. In her growing affection for Orlando, the Queen has placed them in ice – although she will fade, Orlando never will. In the finished film, this relationship reads more as a mark of the Queen's desire for youth writ large than for Orlando themself; the sexual implications are muddy at best.

Orlando's relationship with the Queen in the first draft, however, *is* explicitly sexual, verging on the transactional. After their first meeting, the Queen is active in her pursuit of Orlando. At the banquet, Orlando does not recite poetry to the Queen. Instead, the Queen "often glances at Orlando and at one point we see her tell a courtier to fetch him to her ... occasionally we hear little waves of whispering" (Potter 1988b, SPA0000062). As the scene progresses, "several visual clues indicate that she is increasingly struck by Orlando's looks and demeanor." Then, the transaction occurs: "we see [the Queen] call a courier and sign + seal a document and hand it to Orlando's father: the deeds to the house" (Potter 1988b, SPA0000063). Orlando and the Queen walk together through the grounds of the house, and the Queen says "you will be my ... treasurer ... and steward." In her bedroom that evening, the Queen pulls Orlando in towards her, stroking his head and saying (much in the same way she does in the finished film) "this is my victory ... you will be the son of my old age the limb of my infirmity, my oak tree" (Potter 1988b, SPA0000064). Later, the Queen is obviously jealous when Orlando's affections are paid elsewhere – she smashes a mirror, yelling "treachery!" after she sees a man who may be Orlando kissing another woman (Potter 1988b, SPA0000065). The Queen has, effectively, purchased Orlando from Orlando's father in this first draft, making their love for anyone else a royal offence. There are no demands not to age, no transaction of youth, only an expectation of romantic fidelity to the Queen.

The form that the relationship takes in this draft follows Woolf's text directly and words are often taken wholesale. When the Queen speaks to Orlando, for example, the words are Woolf's: "he was to be the son of her old age," writes Woolf, "the limb of her infirmity; the oak tree on which she leant her degradation" ([1928] 2006, 26). The arc of their relationship, too, is pulled directly from Woolf: the Queen "saw in the mirror ... a boy – could it be Orlando? – kissing a girl – who in the Devil's name was the brazen hussy? Snatching at her golden-hilted sword she struck violently at the mirror" ([1928] 2006, 26). In Potter's first draft, the Queen ruminates on "the treachery of men," verbalizing a hurt that is mirrored in Woolf's novel. In the finished film, however, these words become Orlando's own – refocusing the affective potency of betrayal in a way that centres Orlando's own narrative arc, which was one of the major goals that Potter had set out for herself in adapting Woolf's text.

Potter's first draft also includes scenes with two characters who are missing from the finished film and whose presence (or lack thereof) is of central concern to scholars who have cited the film as a "heterosexualized betrayal of a lesbian love letter" (Fowler 2009, 62). Specifically, the first draft of Potter's screenplay includes narrative threads with the Archduchess Harriet (who, in both this draft of Potter's screenplay and in Woolf's novel, is the Archduke Harry disguised and in drag) and Nell (a prostitute that Orlando picks up once they are a woman). The Archduchess appears in Potter's draft as she does in Woolf's text, after Orlando has had a falling out with the poet Nick Greene (played by Heathcote Williams in the finished film). In Woolf's novel, the Archduchess is described as "a hare whose timidity is overcome with an immense and foolish audacity ... This hare, moreover, was six feet high and wore a headdress into the bargain of some antiquated kind which made her look still taller" ([1928] 2006, 114). Potter consolidates this description in her draft; the Archduchess is an "extremely tall and over-dressed" woman who "starts to swallow her words, breaking occasionally into a nervous laugh" (Potter 1988b, SPA0000674). Feeling suffocated by the Archduchess's attentions, Orlando requests to be sent "abroad." Although Orlando's fleeing of England is correlated with a desire to escape the Archduchess in the first draft, the finished film sees this occur immediately after Orlando's falling out with Nick Greene.

Like Woolf's novel, Potter's first draft has Orlando become an ambassador in Constantinople, where Orlando's transformation to a woman is precipitated by revolution but not specifically by masculine failings to join in the battle, as is the case in the final film. In this draft, Orlando's time in Constantinople (later rewritten to Khiva) functions with little dialogue, moving swiftly between spaces and interactions. This is quite different from the pacing of Potter's finished film, where Orlando's time as an ambassador is marked by a feeling of relaxation and inner peace. In the final version of Potter's film,

Orlando's solitude abroad is interrupted by their first encounter with the Archduke Harry, which occurs *before* Orlando's female transition. While the Archduke does appear in this first draft of Potter's screenplay, it is in accord with Woolf's novel: the Archduchess is revealed to be a man *after* Orlando has been identified as a woman. This simplification of the Archduke/Arch-duchess is in accord with much of the work that Potter's later drafts do, constantly recentring the narrative energy around Orlando. In Woolf's novel, we encounter two sex-related reveals – Orlando's and the Archduke's. Potter's revision forecloses the possibility that supporting characters might distract from Orlando's narrative threads.

Another crucial encounter from Woolf's text remains in the first draft of Potter's script: a scene with Nell, a prostitute that Orlando (at this time a woman, although dressed as a man) picks up in a London square.[5] As they head back to Nell's house (and through a "rather dingy hallway" [Potter 1988c, SPA0000803]), Nell heads behind a curtain to disrobe. Orlando sits on a couch, dressed as a "gallant young man" (Potter 1988c, SPA0000802) although identified at this moment as a woman in both the book and screenplay. Coming out from around the curtain wearing a night gown, Nell "looks at Orlando with a little smile – practiced, professionally coy." Orlando "stands up suddenly, flings off her hat and unbutton[s] her jacket," proclaiming "Nell, I'm not what you think. I'm a woman." This revelation, described in nearly identical prose in Woolf's novel and Potter's first draft of the script, causes Nell to "burst into a roar of laughter" (Potter 1988c, SPA0000804).[6] Nell responds by saying, "I'm by no means sorry to hear it. For the plain Dunstable of the matter is that I'm not in the mood for the society of the other sex tonight."[7] Calling down the hall in a surprisingly masculine tone that highlights her performance of gender, Nell summons her colleagues Kitty and Prue to join for a drink. The four women sit together, analyzing men's expectations of women. In this iteration of the screenplay and novel, the lesbian implications are clear: Orlando (a woman in clearly masculine dress) has actively pursued another woman, literally hiring a prostitute before outing themself as a woman. This is a drastic break from the finished film, in which Orlando's only directly sexual encounter is a seemingly heterosexual one with Shelmerdine (played by Billy Zane).

In Woolf's novel and Potter's first draft, though, the heterosexuality of Orlando and Shelmerdine's relationship is complicated, as there is explicit discussion about the perceived and actual sex of both Orlando and Shelmerdine. Upon first meeting Shelmerdine, Potter notes that he "looks like Sasha" (Potter 1988c, SPA0000818), which was an idea that Potter played with at length in her notes about the film. "Structurally," writes Potter in her notes, Sasha (played by Charlotte Valandrey in the finished film) and Shelmerdine "mirror each other ... cast some twins to play Sasha/Shelmerdine (e.g., the Rossellini twins)" (Potter 1988a, SPA0001922). Potter's first draft sees the interactions between Orlando and Shelmerdine, who fall madly in love upon first meeting, marked by comedy. Just after Orlando and Shelmerdine have exchanged names over breakfast, they kiss. Pulling away from each other, Orlando exclaims "You're a woman, Shel!" And Shelmerdine responds, "You're a man, Orlando!" Putting her hand to her bosom, Orlando says "No! A woman, Shel!" Shelmerdine, putting his hand to his heart, says "A man, Orlando" (Potter 1988c, SPA0000822). This moment – in both Potter's first draft and in Woolf's text – functions as direct acknowledgement of the fluidity of these characters' understandings of each other's sex. Simultaneously, however, this moment also functions to lock Orlando and Shelmerdine into categories, forcing them to recite their sex to one another in binary terms.

At the end of the first draft of Potter's *Orlando*, we are taken to the 1950s and, here, we see the first and only major revision to Woolf's novel. Where Woolf has Orlando give birth to a son at the end of her novel, Potter refuses. In Potter's first draft, we see Orlando in labour but, instead of giving birth in 1928 (where Woolf's novel ends), Potter notes that the "midwife's hairstyle, clothes, and makeup indicate that we are now in the 1950s." Although we do see a pregnant Orlando and although we do see Orlando in labour, Potter's draft omits scenes of their child – we never see a baby being born nor do we hear or see a child at all. This change is a dramatic one for a draft that is, otherwise, quite faithful to its source text.

In Woolf's novel, by giving birth to a son, Orlando is able to regain their family's estate. For scholars of Woolf's novel, this is crucial to the purpose of *Orlando*: Vita Sackville-West, who was Woolf's lover and the inspiration for Orlando, "was born at Knole in 1892 and grew up there, an only child of Victoria and Lionel. She loved Knole but was unable to inherit when her father, the 3rd Lord Sackville died, due to the laws of primogeniture dictating that only men could inherit property" (National Trust, 2015). By giving Orlando a son, Woolf imagines a world where Knole is returned to Vita.

The last time leap of Potter's first draft, however, sees Orlando return to the oak tree where the film began. Now in "the clothes of 1990," Orlando is "apparently asleep, as in scene one" (Potter 1988c, SPA0000847). No child, no reclamation of home, Orlando has fully separated themself from the ties of their former lives. Orlando "takes a breath, her expression fully awake, radiant." The camera "rush[es] up, up and away into darkness and then into clouds and bright, bright whiteness" (Potter 1988c, SPA0000848). While omitting the scene of childbirth may appear to be a large shift away from Woolf's novel, Potter's notes indicate that she may not have understood it as such. In a section of her notes about Sasha and Shelmerdine, Potter writes, "and [Orlando and Shelmerdine's] child? I always forget that Orlando gives birth as a woman. what [*sic*] does this say about how this is written?" (Potter 1988a, SPA0001922). In these notes, Potter writes that "the present moment" of the 1990s "is like a birth. The feeling leading up to it one of blood racing though the veins – a pounding of the heart, expectancy, towards a moment of delivery" (Potter, 1988a, SPA0001918). For Potter, then, this leap forward *is* the metaphoric child that Woolf bestows literally upon Orlando. This abstraction of birth is in accord with gender and literary scholar Erin Kingsley's argument that, for Woolf in her canonical *A Room of One's Own*, "birth … is figurative, controlled, and clean, not literal, bodily, or messy." In this abstraction, Woolf seeks a "bloodless … reproduction of the mind" rather than a literal childbirth (2014). This, I argue, is the kind of "birth" that Sally Potter is working to visualize in her drafts leading up to the published script for the film, although her finished film sees the child made manifest.

To that end, Draft One's total erasure of Orlando's corporeal motherhood is a necessary nuance for the scholarly criticism of Potter's adaptation, which has often taken to task Potter's decision to give Orlando a daughter in the finished film. Film scholars Hollinger and Winterthalter, for example, write that Potter's adaptation of *Orlando* "gives the impression that woman's only 'inheritance' and her path to her 'true self' is through motherhood, symbolized by Orlando's blissful relationship with her female child." This reading of the film is striking given the way that the first draft of Potter's *Orlando* counters this logic, engaging directly with Hollinger and Winterhalter's concerns by erasing Orlando's child from the draft's conclusion. By charting the progression of Potter's adaptation, it is possible to get a sense of the way that Potter landed on a version of *Orlando* that – as Hollinger and Winterhalter's argument demonstrates – could be interpreted as counter to Potter's own thinking about women's relationship to motherhood, property, and intergenerational "inheritance." In this first draft, the 1990s are ripe with potential, rich with a hope for a present and future that can deliver the ecstasy that Orlando desires *without* the tie to childbirth firmly cementing them as a "woman." In so doing, Potter maintains the lesbian/bisexual potential of Woolf's text while beginning to push Woolf's novel forward into a 1990s feminist politics.

PRESENTATION BOOK AND DRAFT TWO: adaptation as a condensation

Just after Potter completed the first draft of the script, she and Tilda Swinton set off to make a "presentation book" for the film. Featuring beautiful colour photographs of Tilda Swinton posing as both the male and female Orlando around the grounds of Knole in the UK (Potter 2019, 34), the presentation book synopsizes Woolf's novel, provides character breakdowns, and highlights the themes and arc of Potter's adaptation. In this document, we see the initial crafting of the visuals that have become emblematic of Potter's *Orlando*; Swinton's performance is strikingly resonant in still image form, but we are also given a story arc that has yet to be impacted by Potter's revisions. Of particular note, this arc still features Queen Elizabeth's mirror-breaking rage, an unmotivated/spontaneous shift in sex in Constantinople, the Archduchess/Archduke's performance of self in drag, and a total lack of conversation about Orlando's pregnancy or labour.

Looking at the presentation book, the first draft of the script from 1988, and her notes, it is clear that Virginia Woolf is the authorial voice of Potter's initial conceptualization of *Orlando*. Yes, Potter is engaged in the act of adaptation, but she is beholden to the flow of Woolf's text and Woolf's imagining of Orlando. Her role is to extend Woolf's vision, translating it for another medium and bringing *Orlando* to the 1990s.[8] However, it is also clear that Potter was debating what the implications of that temporal extension might mean for Orlando's relationship to childbirth. Might she leave Orlando's pregnancy and labour in the film, but leave the child un-visualized? Might she eschew Orlando's pregnancy altogether? If bringing *Orlando* up to Woolf's present (in 1928) meant restoring the family estate to Vita Sackville-West by way of Orlando's son, perhaps Potter's job in taking the film through the 1990s was to remove the need for a child at all.

These questions remain palpable in Potter's second draft (written in 1989 according to SP-ARK), which scales down the overall scope of Woolf's narrative into a more reasonable size for a feature length motion picture. Now typewritten, the revised second draft is roughly the same length (the first draft was 161 handwritten pages, the second draft is 160 typewritten pages), but numerous scenes have been marked for removal. This second draft also begins to root the film in Orlando's explicit and visual point of view, moving away from the narrative style and structure of Woolf's text. To that end, we begin to see Orlando's engagement with the camera in the second draft, although far fewer asides are present than there are in the finished film.

This draft begins, for example, with Orlando under the oak tree, turning to look "directly into the camera" and acknowledging the audience (Potter 1989, SPA0001727). Later, as Orlando and Queen Elizabeth sit at dinner, Potter has begun scratching out references to the Queen's more obvious romantic desire for Orlando. Instead, Potter has handwritten an alternate version of the scene, which places Orlando as the active viewer in their first interaction with the Queen. Instead of having the "intensity of [the Queen's] gaze [indicate] that she is increasingly struck by Orlando's looks and demeanor," Potter has written that "Orlando's eyes flicker up towards Queen Elizabeth. A courtier is tasting Queen Elizabeth's wine before pouring it … Orlando's P.O.V.: Close up of Queen Elizabeth's hands as she snaps her fingers to receive the wine" (Potter 1989, SPA0001730). This is a drastic shift in perspective from Potter's first draft, recentring Orlando as a powerful holder of the gaze. While Orlando and the Queen's relationship progresses along similar lines to those established in Draft One, we begin to see Potter taking small liberties with Woolf's dialogue, signalling a shifting relationship to Woolf's text that becomes more apparent in later drafts.

While the second draft still includes Orlando's relationship with Nell, it shortens their encounter by six pages, signalling the beginning of a shift away from the direct lesbian relationships in Woolf's novel. No longer does Nell call Kitty and Prue in a masculine voice and no longer is there a drink shared between a group of women. Instead, the scene ends with Orlando exposing themself as a woman and Nell responding, "I think I may not be in the mood for the society of the other sex tonight in any case" (Potter 1989, SPA0001866). They toast to the ladies of the new century as Orlando relaxes (Potter 1989, SPA0001872). These changes see Potter beginning to refocus the narrative energy of her adaptation away from the breadth of Woolf's novel, starting instead to focus in on Orlando's own narrative arc and point of view.

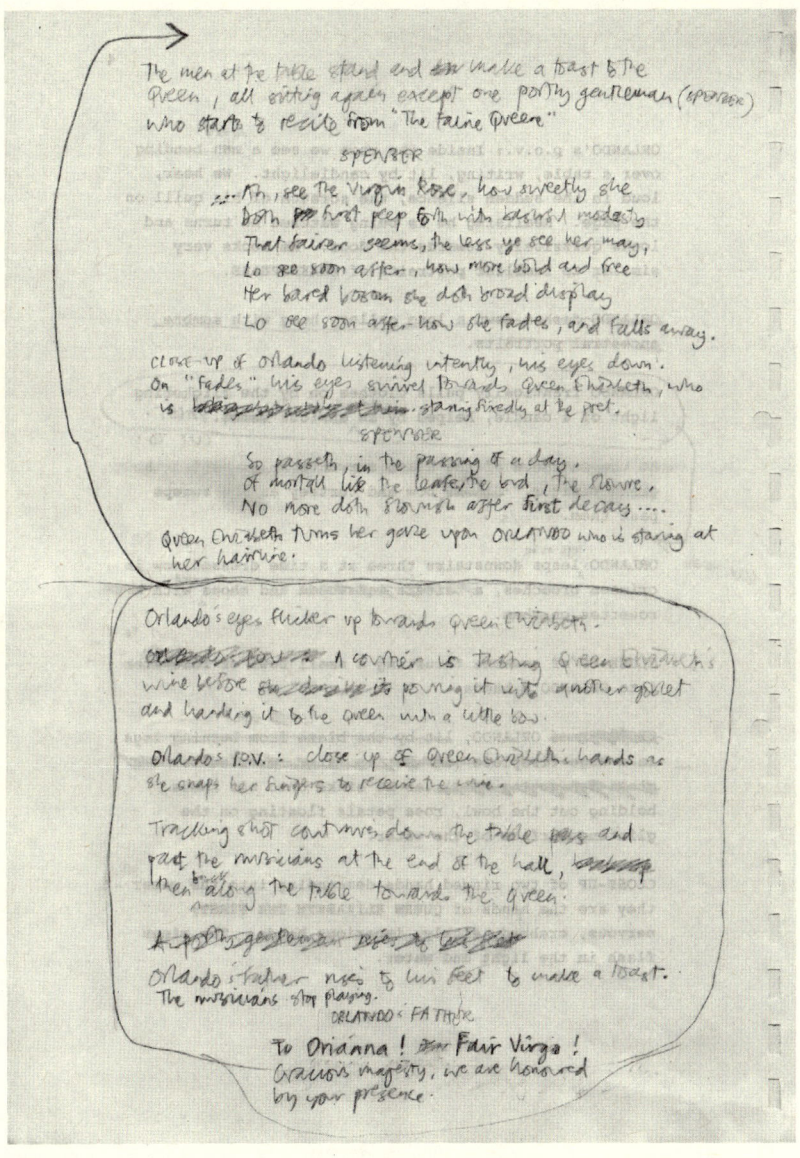

The men at the table stand and make a toast to the
Queen, all sitting again except one portly gentleman (SPENSER)
who starts to recite from "The Faine Queen"

SPENSER

...Ah, see the Virgin Rose, how sweetly she
Doth first peep forth with bashful modesty,
That fairer seems, the less ye see her may;
Lo see soon after, how more bold and free
Her bared bosom she doth broad display
Lo see soon after, how she fades, and falls away.

CLOSE UP of Orlando listening intently, his eyes down.
On "fades" his eyes swivel towards Queen Elizabeth, who
is ~~looking straight at him~~ staring fixedly at the poet.

SPENSER

So passeth, in the passing of a day,
Of mortal life the leafe, the bud, the flowre,
No more doth flourish after first decay....

Queen Elizabeth turns her gaze upon ORLANDO who is staring at
her hairline.

Orlando's eyes flicker up towards Queen Elizabeth.

~~Orlando stares~~ A courtier is tasting Queen Elizabeth's
wine before ~~she drinks it~~ pouring it into another goblet
and handing it to the Queen with a little bow.

Orlando's P.O.V. : close up of Queen Elizabeth's hands as
she snaps her fingers to receive the wine.

Tracking shot continues down the table past and
past the musicians at the end of the hall, ~~towards~~
then ~~along~~ toward the Queen.

~~A portly gentleman rises to his feet~~

Orlando's father rises to his feet to make a toast.
The musicians stop playing.

ORLANDO'S FATHER

To Orianna! ~~our~~ Fair Virgo!
Gracious majesty, we are honoured
by your presence.

Figure 26
Potter's notes on her 1989 draft show an alternate, handwritten version
of the banquet scene.

DRAFT THREE: adaptation as the creation of a new text

Potter's third and longest draft (206 typewritten pages, completed in 1990 according to SP-ARK) sees substantial revisions in the structure, style, dialogue, and narrative arc of the film. Opening in the 1990s and then jumping back in time, the draft bookends the film with its own historical present. Potter also reimagines many of Orlando's relationships, reworking their interactions with Queen Elizabeth I and Nell in ways that diverge from Woolf's text in dramatic ways. A clear shift in authorship is visible through these changes; Draft Three marks a moment in the film's development in which Potter moves from faithfully adapting Woolf's novel to crafting a unique and politically charged reimagining of Woolf's characters.

This version of the script opens with a group of American and Japanese tourists pointing and taking photographs within a "Great English Country House" in 1990. We begin in an alternate version of Potter's frequent end: "Orlando, a tall beautiful woman, her long hair coiled at the nape of her neck, steps silently in front of [a stained glass] window, her profile etched in the red, blue and yellow light." In voiceover, the first words we hear are Orlando's. "What more terrifying revelation can there be than that it is the present moment?" they say. "That we survive the shock at all is only possible because the past shelters us on one side and the future on another" (Potter 1990, SPA0000009). Leaping back in time, we are placed beneath the oak tree, watching Orlando, who is now "a beautiful young man." The voiceover continues, "Time, though it makes animals and vegetables bloom and fade with amazing punctuality, has no such simple effect upon the mind of man. The mind of man, moreover, works with equal strangeness upon the body of time. An hour may be stretched to fifty or a hundred times its clock length; or on the other hand, an hour may be accurately represented on the timepiece of the mind ... by one second" (Potter 1990, SPA0000010). Here, although not as intimate as the asides in the finished film, Potter is actively working to construct an interpersonal relationship between audience and Orlando by way of voiceover, implicating viewers in the link between Orlando's embodiment and existence in "queer time" (as described at the end of chapter 1).

Draft Three also sees a direct turn towards the finished film with respect to the initial moments of Orlando and the Queen's relationship, with Potter reimagining their relationship as fundamentally transactional, although not sexual. Handing over the deed to Orlando's home, the Queen says directly that "in exchange for this little property in perpetuity ... never grow old, Orlando. I tell you young man, after I am gone, I will see to it that you remain exactly as you are now, as long as it pleases me." Clearly not understanding the gravity of this deal, Orlando simply responds "your wit is legendary, your Royal Highness" (Potter 1990, SPA0000017–18). While the Queen's command that Orlando never "grow old" resonates between this draft and the finished film, Draft Three features a drastically different role for the Queen throughout the film. Rather than their relationship ending with her historical death, Draft Three sees the Queen become a constant supernatural presence in Orlando's life.

The first ghostly encounter with the Queen occurs after Orlando has been "betrayed" by Sasha. As Orlando's valets attempt to awaken them from their multiday slumber with song, the audience is launched into a dream state. Orlando is "running silently and very fast through a long, long tunnel between closely planted trees towards Queen Elizabeth who sits stiffly on a felled tree in a clearing in the luminous green light of the forest." The sound of the previous scene has carried over through Orlando's run, but it is quickly interrupted when we "cut to a CLOSE-UP of Queen Elizabeth" (Potter 1990, SPA0001578). This exchange breaks radically from Woolf's text; Potter instead uses the spirit of Queen Elizabeth to direct and mandate Orlando's (preternaturally long) life.

This is not the only time the Queen reappears – the audience enters these dream states with her every time Orlando has a multiday slumber. Through these moments, it is clear that the Queen *is, has been, and will be* the entity that is forcing Orlando's life to take this strange, ageless turn. Draft Three, therefore, is structured around the haunting of Orlando's psyche.

This frequent return to the Queen also makes literal Potter's note that there "had to be reasons – however flimsy – to propel us along a journey based itself on a kind of suspension of disbelief" (Sony Pictures Classics). In this first posthumous return, the Queen tells Orlando that they "will never know death himself" and that she "speak[s] of the perpetual present which you, Orlando, have not yet experienced. For you with your English sorrows are trapped in the past" (Potter 1990, SPA0001580). After reprimanding Orlando, the Queen explains that she is going to "command you back to your cosy oblivion … you are not yet ready to age" (Potter 1990, SPA0001581). This is one of the central changes in Draft Three: Orlando's journey must be (and is repeatedly stated as) a quest to embrace the present. While this concern is also at the core of Potter's final version of the film, there it is executed more subtly. In this draft, we see a larger conceptual shift: rather than being about a reclamation of space for Orlando (or Sackville-West, by association) the film aims to force Orlando to confront the British systems of power with which they are entangled, signified here by the Queen of England.

The Queen next appears after Orlando has fallen asleep amidst a revolution. As in the prior drafts, Orlando has become an ambassador for the King, who wishes to maintain a relationship with the "East." Orlando has relocated to an ambassadorial residence and, after a time serving there, is being celebrated at a lavish and well-attended party in 1670. Mid-party, chaos ensues. As we hear gunshots, we next see Orlando asleep "in a tumble of bedclothes" – Orlando is managing to sleep through a revolution (Potter 1990, SPA0001617). In their interaction with the Queen, which again takes place in the green light of the forest, Orlando speaks of feeling their age, even if they do not look it. While the Queen notes that it has been ninety years since their first meeting, she remarks that Orlando does not look as though they have aged at all. "[I]n my bones," responds Orlando, "I feel I have gone almost as far as I can go" (Potter 1990, SPA0001619). Explaining their current emotional state, Orlando tells the Queen that "I came to Constantinople expecting to feel the greatness of my country reflected in foreign eyes – to feel myself the Lord of my life – in short, to stop feeling like a wretched boy! But what did I find? Those 'ignorant' Turks are more advanced than us in poetry, dance and music ... *and* in philosophy and architecture and, even, dare I say it, in matters of revolution. What else could I do, your Highness, in the face of rebellion, but *sleep*?" (Potter 1990, SPA0001620, emphasis in original).

After all that has led them here and in the face of this revolution, Orlando confesses to the Queen that they are still fixated on Sasha (Potter 1990, SPA0001622). Responding to the weakness she sees in Orlando, the Queen argues that they are "merely the product of [their] heritage with all its strengths and weaknesses" (Potter 1990, SPA0001623). To this, Orlando responds that, "if this is all there is, I have no alternative but to change ... as completely as one *can* change" (Potter 1990, SPA0001624, emphasis in original). And with that, in Draft Three, Orlando awakens from their conversation with Queen Elizabeth to find themself a woman – changed as completely as anyone can change. Orlando has been transformed simply by a realization that they must change – and yet, somehow, they remain just as innocent and naive as they have been all along.

Yet, with regard to Orlando's other relationships, Draft Three pulls away from visualizing them as a perpetual innocent. The love triangle between Euphrosyne, Sasha, and Orlando is fleshed out much more thoroughly in Potter's third draft, pushing the reader's understanding of Orlando in directions that amplify and diminish their perpetual boyishness. For example, a humiliated Euphrosyne ends her relationship with Orlando by commanding them to "indulge your boyish whims! I wonder if you will ever become a man" (Potter 1990, SPA0000044). Although we empathize with Euphrosyne's pain, the joke here, of course, is that Orlando *never will* become a man. This is a striking turn from the finished film, where Euphrosyne and Orlando's falling out ends with Euphrosyne proclaiming that Orlando's actions signify the "treachery of men."

Draft Three also sees a dramatic change in Orlando and Sasha's relationship when Sasha tells Orlando to "taste her ... before [she] is swallowed up once more in [Orlando's] dark imaginings" (Potter 1990, SPA 0000045). In the moments that follow, which do not exist in the finished version of the film, we see Orlando and Sasha in an explicit sex scene, giving the viewer "extreme close ups of Orlando's mouth caressing and nibbling Sasha's body ... Cut in to the extreme close-ups of their love-making is a short sequence of images of a deer stepping incongruously into the Great Hall of Orlando's house" (Potter 1990, SPA 0000045). While much of what follows after the sex scene is a longer (but similar) version of what the audience sees in the finished film, the difference in our understanding of Orlando as virginal is markedly different. Where the finished film works to make murky the distance between romantic relationships and a desire for "company," Orlando clearly understands the sexual implications of romance in Draft Three.

This distinction is only further punctuated by Orlando's encounter with Nell in Draft Three; we witness Potter's authorial voice clearly emerging in this pivotal same-sex encounter. Specifically, in this draft, Orlando is far more hesitant with Nell. When Nell emerges from behind the screen, she beckons Orlando, saying, "Come here – come here. Don't be shy." "Wait – please," Orlando responds with a "nervous expression" (Potter 1990, SPA 0001662). Sitting on the edge of the bed, Orlando sits with their "head down, a hat shielding her face." "Don't be frightened," Nell says, patting the bed "is this your first time?" "No," says Orlando, "flustered, sweating and agitated," "I mean ... it's just that ... I do not require your services. I'm not what you think.... I'm a woman" (Potter 1990, SPA 0001663). Nell responds sarcastically, putting on a "brisk and hard" demeanour. "I have no wish to ...," responds Orlando. "To what? To waste my time?" Nell responds,

To make a fool out of me? … Let me tell you something, young lady. Every day of my working life men come in through that door as one thing and then reveal themselves to be another. Most of them want to hold up a mirror that reflects them back at twice their natural size. Some want me to make them feel small and helpless to relieve them of the burdens of high office. But mostly they come in as men and leave as men. But you … Did you just happen to be strolling round town in fancy dress … and want to test the effectiveness of your disguise on an innocent working girl? … Though I suppose, come to think of it, there's worse disguises than being dressed as a man …. Being dressed as a woman for instance. Especially if you are one. (Potter 1990, SPA0001665–6)

At this point, "Nell bursts into self-mocking laughter, then she takes Orlando's hand and pulls her across the room to the bed, friskily unbuttons Orlando's jacket and lets down Orlando's hair." "There," says Nell, "let me look at you" (Potter 1990, SPA0001666). "I never realized – I never guessed – that it would feel like this," responds Orlando (Potter 1990, SPA0001667). Sitting with Nell, Orlando begins to cry; Nell slips Orlando into bed and then gets in beside them. "Can I stay with you for this hour?" Orlando asks. "In one hour it will be the new century," Nell responds. "Cry your heart out, dear, for if you think things are bad now then they will surely get worse." With this, Orlando cries "harder and harder. Intercut with her tears and Nell's kisses and caresses are a sequence of images of the coming of the Victorian era, the overall tone of which is fecund, elaborate, adorned and damp" (Potter 1990, SPA0001668).

Working to reconcile the lesbian feminist potential of Orlando with her own interest in a story about genderlessness, Potter's voice is so articulate and clear in this scene. Orlando's chance to feel melancholy for all that has been lost in youth – that is, the chance to cry – is lucid in this meaningful scene, later cut from the script.

Asleep in Nell's arms, we launch into Orlando's last dream encounter with Queen Elizabeth. A tired, frustrated Queen continues to accuse Orlando of "whining," but Orlando is beginning to take control. The Queen accuses Orlando of sleeping through the "*industrial* revolution," but Orlando quickly snaps back, "I sleep as a woman in the arms of a woman" (Potter 1990, SPA0001672, emphasis in original). In their last encounter, Orlando is far braver and more vocal than they have been before. When the Queen critiques Orlando's social and economic position, Orlando responds by reminding the Queen of her own privilege, wealth, and status. Warning Orlando that this is the last time they will meet, the Queen says that she is "resigning both from my position in the national psyche and from my place in your soul." Emphasizing the fact that the Queen has been Orlando's longest relationship throughout this draft, Orlando responds that, if the Queen is leaving them, then they will need to go find a mate (Potter 1990, SPA0001674).

In perhaps the most didactic moment of Potter's third draft, she lays Orlando's feelings bare. "When I was a man and everyone would listen," Orlando says to the Queen, "I had nothing to say." But now, as a woman, "I know that I wish to speak but have lost my voice and if I find it, I fear that no-one will listen." "Hah!" responds Queen Elizabeth, "I resign! And so, eventually, will you." "From what, Elizabeth?" responds Orlando. "From what?" "From your class," the Queen responds (Potter 1990, SPA0001676). In adapting Woolf, Potter has been working to move Orlando beyond their fixation with their family's estate rather than working to restore it to them.

While this extended spirit-role for the Queen only exists in the third draft of the script, it is a telling and dramatic beat in Potter's evolution of *Orlando* away from an adaptation that prioritizes a faithful translation of Woolf's text to the screen. Potter's dedication to Woolf's novel is like Orlando's fixation with their estate: to grow in the present, we must move beyond the past.

DRAFT FOUR: adaptation as a controlled burn

Draft Four of Sally Potter's *Orlando*, completed in 1991 according to SP-ARK (about a year before production began) starts with handwritten notes and drawings. On the cover page, Potter has written "ORLANDO AS MAN predominantly left axis of screen" and "ORLANDO AS WOMAN predominantly right axis." Above these notes, Potter has drawn a diagram of a tree on a hillside with notes that the "sky [is] b+w" and the "landscape [is] col[our]" (Potter 1991, SPA0001337). Beginning to leave herself additional notes that would be central for her work with the film's cinematographer, this draft of the script is rich with these sorts of handwritten diagrams and illustrations.

Draft Four once again begins with Orlando under the oak tree. Orlando is moving their lips "as if memorising some verse, his eyes closed but visibly flickering behind his eyelids ... Orlando opens his eyes, looks directly into the camera, and smiles." In this draft, we begin to see an intimate relationship between Orlando and the film's audience being developed through these turns towards the camera. To camera, Orlando says, "Right. I stand there – proud. I show my legs off – they're rather fine – I smile – I like sugar – that's good – At your service, Majesty – Can we have the house? No. Whatever you do – *don't* mention the house ... Just read the poem – 'Ah – see the virgin rose'" (Potter 1991, SPA0001338, emphasis in original). The film jumps, as it does in the finished film, to servants carrying torches. A handwritten note says "Queen boat?" (Potter 1991, SPA0001339), which is then followed up by shots of the Queen in the "royal barge" (Potter 1991, SPA0001340). The opening of this draft is a clear precursor of the grand entrance that Potter ultimately crafts for Crisp's "Queen" in the finished film, but places more emphasis on Orlando's emotional investment in acquiring the deed to their family's home.

In this draft, the scene in the banquet hall is strikingly in line with Potter's final version; the Queen, as she does in the final film, stops Orlando's recitation of *The Faerie Queene* midstream (it has been read by other characters in

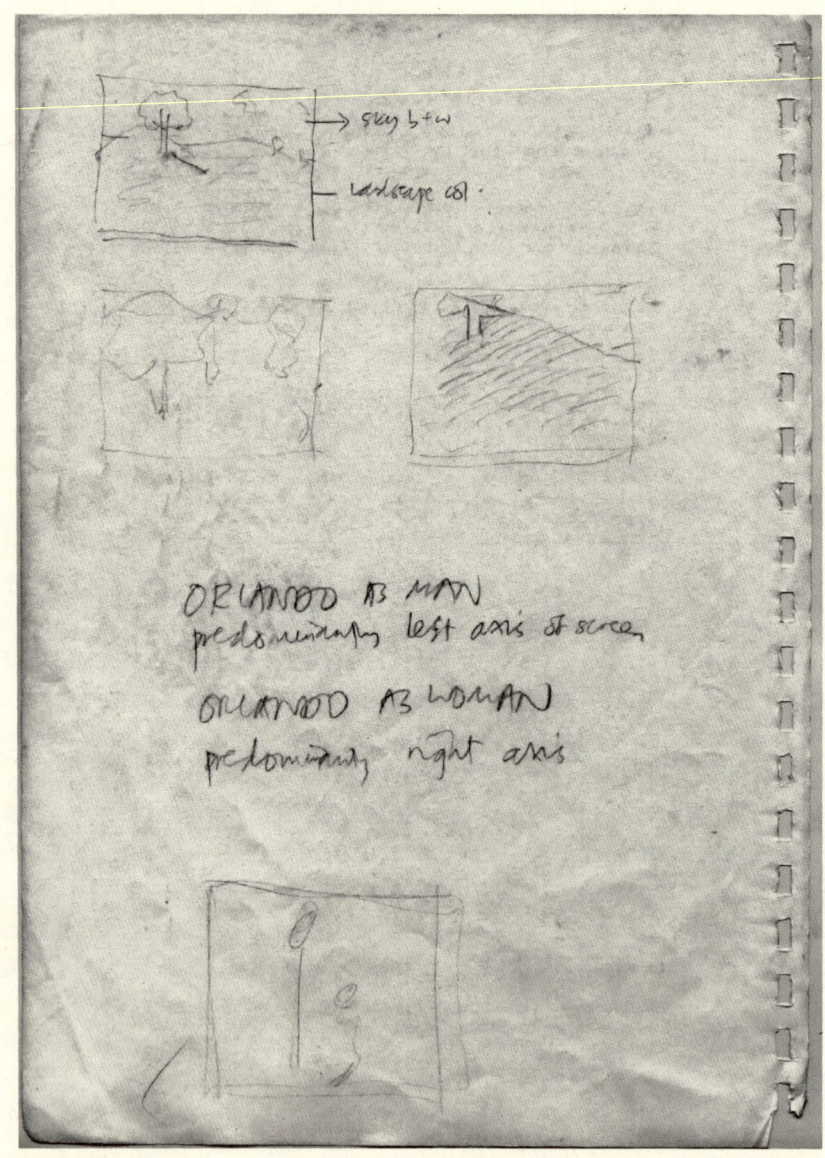

Figure 27

A handwritten note in Potter's 1991 draft suggests "ORLANDO AS MAN predominantly left axis of screen" and "ORLANDO AS WOMAN predominantly right axis."

prior drafts), explaining that the poem is "not a worthy topic from one so clearly in the bloom of youth to one who would desire it still" (Potter 1991, SPA0001344). The one considerable difference in the initial encounter between the Queen and Orlando is a dance between the two that follows Orlando's recitation. Potter writes that Orlando "lifts her, again and again obediently, his face flushed and perspiring" while the Queen's "face has cracked into a smile, revealing grotesquely discolored teeth" (Potter 1991, SPA0001346). Lying in bed after their dance, Orlando again speaks to the camera/audience: "Okay. So it was the wrong poem. But – no – definitely – I'm a hit. Really – and I like *her*. Yes. Great dancer. Very energetic. Lots of pep. Can we have the house?" (Potter 1991, SPA0001348, emphasis in original).

On their walk the next day, the Queen suggests that she may "borrow [Orlando's] pretty visage at court" but that "we would ask something of you." "Anything," responds Orlando, "anything at all" (Potter 1991, SPA0001349). "Do not fade," the Queen says. "Fade?" "Do not wither." Orlando laughs. "Do not *grow old*," the Queen explains. In what follows, the audience is presented with multiple scenes of the Queen doting on Orlando, presenting them with a garter, and stroking their face. Only then, six scenes later, does the Queen tuck the deed to the house into Orlando's garter. In response, Orlando addresses the camera/audience and says, "You know – you try your hand at wit, and being dashing. And you know – making her laugh – or just *listening*. She likes that a lot. And then – what does it? Legs. A pair of legs" (Potter 1991, SPA0001355–6, emphasis in original). In these asides, Potter grapples with Orlando's youth and naivety, but in a way that allows her to toy with childish understandings of what it means to *be* a man – and to be a man in relationships with women. Orlando's aside to camera makes transparent that they are using their boyish charms to hustle the Queen for the deed; Orlando is *working* when they are with the Queen. No falling out, no mirror breaking, no "betrayal" or "treachery," Draft Four is the first in which Orlando's devotion to the Queen (however obligatory, feigned, or bought) remains through her death.

In Draft Four, queerness abounds in Orlando's first interaction with Sasha. Described as a "boyish" figure who immediately catches Orlando's eye, it is clear in Potter's screen direction that Orlando is entranced by Sasha from the moment they see her. But, when Orlando asks a lord-in-waiting who this person is, Orlando says, "Who *is* that boy?" Orlando is shocked to learn that this beautiful, boyish figure is in fact a "princess" (Potter 1991, SPA0001361, emphasis in original). By making the gender confusion explicit here, Potter is inviting queer readings of this relationship. Obviously enamoured, Orlando believes that they are lusting for another boy – the fact that Sasha is ultimately revealed to be a woman does not undo the queer work that Potter has established. Emphasizing this, Orlando addresses the camera/audience during dinner with Sasha and her accompanying ambassadors, saying, "This is the *most* beautiful, the *most* gorgeous and the *most* terrific person I have *ever*, *ever*, *ever* seen in my life. Compared with which, quite frankly, every other woman I have *ever* met is – well" (Potter 1991, SPA0001365, emphasis in original). As Orlando and Sasha continue their romp together, escaping the crowds of the dinner party, Orlando explains to Sasha, "You know, Sasha, sometimes you fill me with the strangest curiosity." "Why?" Sasha responds. "You see, I thought at first that you must be a boy ... But of course, no boy ever had a mouth like yours, nor eyes which looked as if they had been fished from the bottom of the sea" (Potter 1991, SPA0001370–1). In these brief moments, we understand that Orlando is open to the idea of pursuing either men or women; they lust for this *person*, regardless of their sex. In Woolf's novel, this is a moment that theorist George Piggford argues is about Orlando's desire for "a figure of ambiguous gender" (1997, 53).

Furthermore, Orlando's argument to Sasha that "no boy ever had a mouth like yours, nor eyes" is a wonderfully queer one within the scope of Potter's film. After all, Swinton is playing a male Orlando about whom we could say the exact same thing. This gender play is heightened in Draft Four, requiring us to constantly question our interpretation of Swinton's body on screen. While these lines do not survive into Potter's finished film, as I discuss in chapter 1 of this book, the queer energy and potential does. In Potter's hands, Swinton's image is at once feminine, masculine, female, male, boyish – it is forever in the in-between.

These conversations about the social expectations of gender are also elaborated upon in Orlando's relationship with Nick Greene. After Greene leaves, Orlando is standing, brooding towards the camera, hurt, full of rage, with a bonfire burning behind them. This is the point at which the finished film ends the scene – Orlando communicates to the audience with their eyes, but does not speak. In Draft Four, we are given an additional to-camera aside in which Orlando's youthfulness and hurt is punctuated: "No – it's great. Really. Because I have no ambitions – no really – none at all – to be an artist. Patron? Terrific. Great. He deserves it. Witty man! He's got a point. I've got money – he's got the talent. Makes sense. Absolutely. Besides – he's done me a favor. Reminded me – I'd almost forgot! My duty! As a man. I mean – there's times you have to take up your *career*. As a *man*. A man of action. Destiny and all that. Poetry? Hah. Travel! Abroad. As far as possible" (Potter 1991, SPA0001412, emphasis in original). While this monologue gives us a sense of why Orlando agrees to pay Greene and why Orlando then moves to become an ambassador, it also dilutes the rage that is palpable in Potter's finished film. While Potter moves to make Orlando's internal dialogue explicit in Draft Four, she then pulls back towards simple, knowing glances between the audience and Orlando in the finished film.

By reducing the amount of dialogue that Orlando delivers directly to us while maintaining their glances to camera, Potter allows us to *read into* rather than *be told about* Orlando's headspace. This reading into provides a productive potential for those who wish to interpret the film in queer ways, but it also allows the film's nonverbal moments to fester with radical potential. Where Orlando's to-camera aside about Greene in Draft Four places their hurt as concretely about his cruel poetry, Orlando's silent brooding in the finished film allows the audience the space to understand their emotional pain far more complexly.

Draft Four also provides Potter's first homo/social male relationship form-
ing between Orlando and the Khan (played by Lothaire Bluteau in the finished
film). This relationship, which is instrumental to Orlando's change of sex in
Potter's finished film, is totally lacking from all earlier drafts. In Draft Four,
Potter refocuses Orlando's time as an ambassador, moving the location of
their ambassadorial duties from Constantinople to Khiva. In this shift, Potter
also changes the narrative arc of this episode from one primarily about Orlando's ambassadorial duties to one centred around their relationship with
the Khan, having both characters speak of their "brotherly love" as "brothers
in the flesh" (Potter 1991, SPA0001428). This draft also sees a shift in Orlando's
relationship with the Archduke/Archduchess – namely that the Archduchess
has now been removed completely. In Draft Four as in the finished film, we
are first introduced to the Archduke Harry when he interrupts Orlando's
steam bath in Khiva. There to celebrate Orlando's ten years as ambassador,
the Archduke bursts in on Orlando's solitude, bringing the rude reminder of
England back into Orlando's life. When Orlando places their hand on the
Archduke's arm in response, the Archduke is flustered, blushing and jumping
back. As Orlando and the Archduke explore the city's streets, Orlando explains
to the Archduke that "the Khan is a *very* interesting person" (Potter 1991,
SPA0001434, emphasis in original). Orlando's time as an ambassador is an
important break from prior drafts – Draft Four is the first in which the
"East" allows Orlando a swirling mix of homoerotic energy and interest.
While Orlando is clearly enchanted with the Khan, Harry is quickly becoming
enamoured with Orlando.

Potter also reimagines the party that the Archduke throws for Orlando in
this draft. As is the case in the finished film, partygoers do not arrive and, instead, we are left focusing on the relationships between Orlando, the Khan,
and the Archduke. As the guards break up the party, Orlando is ushered towards a confrontational conversation with the Khan. Explaining the situation,
the Khan says, "Orlando – the Russians are coming. Peter's army is at the City
Wall. Will you help?" "You wish me to take arms … against the *Russians*?" re-

Figure 28
The Archduke Harry is enamoured with Orlando while in Khiva.

sponds Orlando (Potter 1991, SPA0001440, emphasis in original). By making
the link with Russia direct, here, Potter has Orlando choosing between relationships (with the Khan and Sasha, specifically). In so doing, the line between
romantic and political relationships is further muddled. Setting up a love triangle that mirrors Orlando's relationship with Sasha and Euphrosyne, Potter
is able to craft a moment in which Orlando, the Khan, and the Archduke's
desire for the "brotherly love" of "the flesh" is one that is simultaneously innocent, earnest, and deeply imperialist – at once about sex and country.
Thrown into battle with men falling and dying around them, Orlando has
chosen their relationship with the Khan over their memory of Sasha.

This choice is transformational for Orlando in both Draft Four and in the finished film – it is a moment when Orlando is confronted with violence and forced to decide how to respond – but it is executed differently. In the finished film, we immediately see Orlando walk away from the battle (both literally and metaphorically), looking straight into the lens. In Draft Four, Orlando turns towards the camera in the midst of the battle, telling us, "*everything until now has been a rehearsal for this. This is the big one. The showdown. Am I prepared to kill and be killed? Is that what being a man is all about? Ultimately? Is that the choice? The test? It's not easy … But what an opportunity. There's no doubt – It's a great opportunity for an identity crisis*" (Potter 1991, SPA0001444, emphasis in original). Only then does Orlando "[walk] away from the battle through the streets as a stream of men rush in the opposite direction" (Potter 1991, SPA0001446). In this moment, like in the moments after Greene's scathing criticism of their poetry, Orlando's asides to camera serve to make things plain for the audience. By asking the question, Orlando's aside implies that "kill[ing] and be[ing] killed" *is* the test of manhood; violence is the testing ground. If Orlando cannot take that test, Orlando cannot be a "man."

The purposeful clarity of these asides changes our understanding of Orlando's transition to "woman." As Orlando awakens after their slumber, they drop their robe in front of the mirror, exposing the body of "a beautiful woman." Turning "and look[ing] innocently into the camera, inviting our acceptance," Orlando says, "So? You knew it all along. Great. But I mean – can you understand my position? The point is this – I was a man until the age of thirty – give or take a couple of hundred years – yes! Yes! It hasn't escaped my notice! And then I became a woman. Same person! Oh yes! Absolutely. No difference. No difference at all … Just a different sex" (Potter 1991, SPA0001448). While this aside ends as it does in the finished film, Orlando's acknowledgment here that the audience "knew" they were a woman "all along" is a drastic break from where Potter lands in the finished film.

This moment in Orlando's dialogue is complex with regard to the film's queerness. On the one hand, by acknowledging that the audience has known Swinton's own sex from the beginning (and, to some extent, Orlando's by association), Potter works to acknowledge the way in which Swinton's casting does code Orlando as "female." In so doing, Orlando's acknowledgment of this allows us to very easily think backwards to their relationship with Sasha, for example, in queer terms. "Aha!" we might say, "Orlando has been a woman 'all along' and, therefore, 'her' relationship with Sasha was, in fact, a lesbian one."

This draft also encourages the audience to think cyclically during the Archduke's marriage proposal and in Orlando's first interactions with Shelmerdine. When the Archduke proposes, the Archduke's notion that Orlando belongs to him because he "adore[s]" them strikes Orlando as painfully similar to their own words to Sasha. Turning towards the camera, Orlando says, "Oh my God. Sasha. Is this how … It brings things into focus." Then, clearly responding to the Archduke as much as to a prior version of themself, Orlando responds that the Archduke's adoration "does not make me your *possession*" (Potter 1991, SPA0001478–9, emphasis in original). Similarly, when Orlando meets Shelmerdine in Draft Four, they turn towards the camera and tell us "I knew he'd come! The man of my dreams … I've waited a long time for this" (Potter 1991, SPA0001499). This to-camera articulation of their enthusiasm for Shelmerdine reinforces the sense that Orlando is and has always been a woman. Furthermore, Orlando's positioning of Shelmerdine as the "man of my dreams" is in stark contrast to their articulation of Sasha as a "boy" earlier in this draft. Orlando – who we might argue to be a perpetual woman in this draft – has grown from desiring "boys" to "men."

These orchestrated moments work to position the roles for "men" and "women" in far clearer terms than in Potter's finished film. In both Woolf's novel and Potter's finished film, when Orlando is told that they have officially lost their home, Shelmerdine explains that they are now "free." In Draft Four, unlike in the finished film, this develops into a heartbreaking argument for Orlando in which it is obvious that they still hold their home (and thereby their position in an imperialist British history) dear. Shelmerdine, chastising Orlando, responds, "when the Queen handed you the deeds to this house – quite unearned I think – where was I? And all the others like me? Have all other histories been obliterated by your noble conceit?" (Potter 1991, SPA0001502). "Stay and stagnate in the past – or leave and live," Shelmerdine commands. "The choice is yours! ... The future is in your hands." "You heard what they said," responds Orlando. "The future is in my *body*." "The future is in your *mind*!" responds Shelmerdine (Potter 1991, SPA0001503, emphasis in original).

Shelmerdine attempts to shake Orlando into the present, to address the inequality that led them to this moment, but he is unable to wrest Orlando from their historical and cultural baggage. In the published screenplay for *Orlando*, Potter describes her reimagining of the Shelmerdine/Orlando relationship as one that refocuses Shelmerdine as the bearer of the "romantic and revolutionary view of the beginning of the American dream ... Shelmerdine functions as the one looking to the future while Orlando is apparently stuck in the past" (Potter and Woolf 1994, xii). This distinction becomes a clear strategy for Potter in Draft Four, where the split between the past and future is articulated in terms of the body and mind. Orlando's statement that "the future is in my *body*" demonstrates that they continue to be entangled in the imperialist logic that understands their female body to be the bearer of children and, thereby, their only link with the future. In so correlating their future with their body/ability to bear children, Orlando understands their relationship to the future through the language of the British officers who strip them of their home. In a surprising turn, Shelmerdine comes to represent a feminist future that stands in contrast to British imperialism. Shelmerdine pushes Orlando to embrace a logic that, as I will explain in the final chapter of this book, is very much in league with Woolf's argument in her 1928 text *A Room of One's*

Own: women, like men, need freedom from the distractions of childbearing and rearing in order to embrace the future of intellectual pursuits.

As Orlando and Shelmerdine leave each other in Draft Four, Orlando looks "grimy, cold and confused" (Potter 1991, SPA0001505). They turn towards the camera and quietly tell us that "this is … good. Really good. I mean it. What an opportunity! To completely re-think. The entire basis of my entire existence. Again" (Potter 1991, SPA0001506). Then, in a complete break from previous or future drafts, Orlando does something radical: they literally light the house on fire. They "run through the house carrying a flaming torch and [begin] to set light to tapestries, furniture, paintings. Soon the whole house is ablaze." In this moment, we also realize that Orlando is "heavily pregnant." As Orlando turns their back on the "blazing house in the distance … smoke curls into the sky." As the world around them burns, the camera cuts to a shot inside an ambulance: Orlando is giving birth. Immediately, we jump back in time in "glittering black and white" (Potter 1991, SPA0001508).

First, we cut to 1850: "Orlando now leaps onto the horse with Shelmerdine, and waves goodbye ecstatically to the Great House, as they gallop off together into the storm." Then to 1750: "Orlando throws back a wedding veil, her face radiant, as a shower of rose petals falls over her head. She turns, lifts her face and kisses … the Archduke Harry as wedding bells chime and people cheer." Then to 1710: "Orlando takes a gun and takes his place by the Khan's side." Rushing into battle, the Khan is "struck by a sword" and then Orlando is "struck down, and falls limply across the Khan's body." Then to 1650: "Orlando is scribbling furiously, with ink-stained fingers … a sea of rejected pages lies at his feet" (Potter 1991, SPA0001509). Nick Greene sits "amongst the sea of papers, reading a manuscript with obvious approval and delight." Then to 1610: "Orlando and Sasha stand, side by side on the deck of the ship, looking back at the river as the ice breaks and the water swirls behind them." Then to 1600: "Queen Elizabeth is handing Orlando the deeds to the house … Orlando stops her, pushing her hand away … Orlando struggles with the

Queen, pushing her hand away repeatedly, until the deeds fall into the fire, bursting into flames." Then to 1576: "Someone is fanning Orlando's mother's face as she lies groaning in labour, tossing and turning amongst the pillows of the great four-poster bed" (Potter 1991, SPA0001511). "It's a girl," the nurse announces (Potter 1991, SPA0001513).

We then begin to jump forward. First, we're transported to 1944: "Orlando, lying on a hospital bed" has just given birth to a girl. Then, we jump forward to 1950: we see a "close-up of a foot starting a motorbike. It is Orlando. Her small daughter sits in the open side-car wearing a huge crash-helmet." The two drive up towards the Great House, which "is entirely covered in scaffolding and flapping plastic, only the vaguest outline of the former house now visible" (Potter 1991, SPA0001513). Just then, we jump forward again, this time to the present day: "tourists are moving through the rooms, past 'Do Not Touch' notices, pointing and taking photographs. Orlando stands with her daughter amongst the crowd." Beneath the oak tree, Orlando's daughter is "taking photographs of insects in the grass." A trumpet sounds and "Orlando opens her eyes and looks directly into the camera." In their final aside to the audience, Orlando says, "so there you have it. Four hundred years to learn – What? To let go of the past. I thought – I thought – inheritance guaranteed my immortality. You know – if not me – my heirs – same thing really. In which case – without land and house – What am I? Mortal! A member of the human race! So simple. Amazing how terrifying it is really. Coming into the present. Like being born really. Or dying" (Potter 1991, SPA0001515 and SPA0001517). With that, "Orlando opens her mouth and takes a breath, her expression fully awake, radiant. As she does so, all sound ceases" (Potter 1991, SPA0001517).

Through this morphing, time-bending conclusion, Potter takes the chance to undo one of the elements that she found the most troubling about Woolf's original text: that in Woolf's version Orlando ends up with a son and, therefore, with the house. In so doing, Orlando perpetuates the masculinist, imperialist system that robbed them of their home in the first place. So Mayer has argued that Potter allows Charlotte Bronte's *Jane Eyre* to "haunt" the 1992 draft of the screenplay both in Shelmerdine's introduction and in the draft's dramatic conclusion. In Mayer's comparison, Orlando "become[s] the mad-woman in the attic in a rage of gender and class consciousness" (2008, 41). Potter is able to harness that "rage" in this draft in past-altering ways, allowing Orlando the chance to torch their family home, refuse the deed, go back in time, and be born a woman. Unlike in the finished film, Orlando never finishes writing *The Oak Tree* in this draft of the screenplay. With no manuscript and no son, Orlando is freed from the past.

In this draft, there is far more clarity in terms of Orlando/Swinton's status as "woman." For all of the feminist potential of these revisions, articulating Orlando as a "woman" in this way would have had the potential to fix our understanding of Swinton's body within the world of the film. By removing these references to Orlando's status as a perpetual "woman," though, Potter allows her finished film (perhaps less obviously lesbian feminist) to be all the more queer. Instead of the audience being able to clearly map past relationships onto Orlando's obviously female body, we are encouraged to remain in a questioning headspace. In Potter's finished film, it is not clear whether or not Orlando has been a "woman" the whole time. As such, the audience has to work to understand the relationships in the film as either heterosexual or not – it simply is not clear. To my mind, it is this exact murkiness that makes Potter's film so wonderfully queer, even when the relationships are less obviously lesbian than in Woolf's novel or Potter's earlier drafts.

It is unusual to have such comprehensive access to early screenplay drafts of an adapted work. To that end, Potter's SP-ARK has proven to be an incredible resource in my ability to chart the evolution of her film from a celebrated lesbian novel to a markedly queer film. Encountering these drafts, I find myself struck by the way in which Potter went about adapting Woolf's text, starting faithfully and slowly working her way towards an incorporation of her own politics and priorities. While this process takes the most dramatic shifts away from Woolf's novel in drafts three and four, we do see Potter easing back towards Woolf's text in her final edit of the film. In the version of the film that premiered at film festivals in 1993, Orlando's to-camera addresses are cut down dramatically, Orlando's relationship to female embodiment is far murkier and complex, and Orlando's home (although not belonging to Orlando at the end of the film) has not literally been burned to the ground.

Through this adaptation process, Potter was able to craft a film that revels in the in-between. While the shifts away from Woolf's text ultimately eliminated the romantic connections that are clearly and explicitly lesbian, the film instead allows us to question the surface level heterosexuality of nearly every relationship in which Orlando is engaged. It is exactly this ambiguity that allows Potter to take a novel written as a lesbian love letter and wind up with a film deeply queer in its position to sex, gender, embodiment, and time. Thirty years after the film's release, that ambiguity speaks more to our current notion of nonbinary gender and queerness than Potter could have possibly imagined in the late 1980s and early 1990s.

Chapter 3

in pursuit of a "common sentence"
(*Orlando* alongside *A Room of One's Own*)

As I described in this book's introduction, I often teach Sally Potter's *Orlando* in both my undergraduate Introduction to Cinema and Queer Cinema courses. Without fail, there is a consistent break in how our conversations proceed and, each semester, I find myself hypothesizing why *Orlando* seems so challenging for straight, cisgender young men. Why is Tilda Swinton's nude body (which, in any other film, would likely be understood as erotic and sexualized) so baffling and uncomfortable? Why does Orlando's change of sex pose such a blockage for some viewers when many willingly embrace other superhuman transformation narratives? (*Spiderman*'s Peter Parker transforms into a spider-human hybrid on screen with little pushback regarding his transition's believability.)

The answer, I think, lies in the ways that Potter's adaptation of *Orlando* engages with Woolf's *A Room of One's Own*, a theoretical essay about the role of women in fiction, which was first presented as two papers read at the Arts Society at Newnham College and the Odtaa at Girton College in October 1928 (the same month that *Orlando* was published). In *Room*, Woolf playfully engages with the history (or lack thereof) of women's writing. Over the course of her essay, Woolf imagines a tragic sister for Shakespeare, explains the conditions under which Jane Austen and the Brontë sisters wrote, and, ultimately, pushes young female writers to embrace any subject matter that interests them. Perhaps most importantly, Woolf uses *Room* to argue that a woman "must have money and a room of her own if she is to write fiction" ([1929] 2019, 1). Specifically, she should make £500 per year, which was the amount that Woolf had been receiving as an annual (and perpetual) inheritance from a deceased aunt. For Woolf, these material conditions and privileges are key. Unlike men, who often steal away to their private studies to write, women are only given access to the busy, common drawing rooms of the home. Women's writing, when it is possible at all in those spaces, becomes fractured in a way that is markedly different from men's because they are, quite literally, interrupted. "If a woman wrote," Woolf explains, "she would have to write in the common sitting-room ... 'women never have an half hour ... that they can call their own' – she was always interrupted" ([1929] 2019, 54). For Woolf in *A Room of One's Own*, this is the fundamental problem: in order for women to have a role in fiction, they need uninterrupted space in which to do the work of writing.

Based on notes available via SP-ARK, it is clear that Potter read and took notes on *A Room of One's Own* while adapting *Orlando*, which morphed from a faithful adaptation of Woolf's novel to a unique reimagining of Woolf's central characters (Potter, n.d.). While the links between the two remain abstract in her production documents, I want to use this chapter to argue that Potter's *Orlando* entwines itself with Woolf's *A Room of One's Own* in two distinct ways: Potter engages thematically with the arguments of Woolf's essay while simultaneously translating Woolf's desire for women to have the space to craft their own written language – as she articulates at length in *A Room of One's Own* – into a gentle cinematic language.[1]

The need for (literal) space in which creative labour can occur is a connection between Potter's oeuvre and Woolf's *A Room of One's Own* that other scholars have insightfully linked, albeit in different ways than I pursue in this chapter. For example, in her monograph analyzing Potter's career, film scholar Catherine Fowler sees Woolf's arguments echoed in the narratives and dialogue of films like *Thriller* (Sally Potter, 1979), in which there is a "comparable exploration of the inaccessibility of certain spaces to women and the roles that they have been assigned" as well as "another echo of Woolf's astonishment at the rarity with which novels by women depict women as friends rather than rivals" (2009, 38). Fowler also argues that "Potter's working practices, and her resulting films, represent an exploration of the problems encountered by women who seek a room of their own" (2009, 25). Fowler sees this relationship playing out directly in Potter's equitable, female-driven sets for films like *The Gold Diggers* (Sally Potter, 1983), which featured an exclusively female crew where all cast and crew were paid equally.

I agree with Fowler that these are some of the central questions Potter grapples with in her body of work. However, I want to push this a step further, hearing echoes of Woolf's *A Room of One's Own* in the way that Potter crafts a unique cinematic language in *Orlando*. In Woolf's argument, one of the most foundational challenges that face women who sit to write is that, "when they [come] to set their thoughts on paper," they have "no tradition behind them." She has "no common sentence to use" (Woolf [1928] 2006, 62). Unlike male writers who can continually share and modify a "common sentence," thereby making their own version of something that has already been written by other men thousands of times before, the only option for women has been to try to borrow language from men.[2] As such, Woolf argues that most women who have managed to write at all have taken up masculine forms of writing – namely, the novel. In Woolf's argument, this gendered tension only compounds when women's writing, often about "the feelings of women in a drawing-room," is treated as "trivial" when compared to that of men writing of war and other "important" topics (Woolf [1929] 2019, 60).

But how does one go about crafting that "common sentence"? As Woolf ends *A Room of One's Own*, she urges young women to write, and to write "all kinds of books, hesitating at no subject however trivial or however vast" ([1929] 2019, 89). The answer must be to write without the shame or concern that past female writers had been taught to internalize. "If you would please me," Woolf implores: "you would write books of travel and adventure, and research and scholarship, and history and biography, and criticism and philosophy and science. By doing so, you will certainly profit the art of fiction. For books have a way of influencing one another ... Moreover, if you consider any great figure of the past, like Sappho, like the Lady Murasaki, like Emily Brontë, you will find that she is an inheritor as well as an originator, and has come into existence because women have come to have the habit of writing naturally; so that even as a prelude to poetry such activity on your part would be invaluable" ([1929] 2019, 89). This is one of the central appeals of Woolf's *A Room of One's Own*: write so that we will have a shared history of women's writing. Write so that other women can have a "common sentence" from which to draw. Only in so doing might we come to know the syntax of that "common sentence," a sentence that need not be structured in the form of its masculine predecessors.

This, I believe, is what makes Sally Potter's *Orlando* such a magical, beautiful film to some and so deeply confusing to others. In the words of So Mayer, the film "present[s] an alternate science fiction: a feminist speculative fiction that explores the tropes of bodily and cultural adaptation, while experimentation with the medium itself replaces experimental science within the narrative" (2008, 39). In so doing, Potter's *Orlando* engages with style and characters in familiar ways while challenging the syntax of genre. Although Potter's film follows the trajectory of a three-act narrative feature film (perhaps we can call that the "masculine cinematic form"), Potter's *Orlando* takes Woolf's task seriously by grappling with the familiar cultural myths that Mayer alludes to, employing a cinematic grammar that thwarts the audience's ability to fetishize the bodies of her characters.

Reaching towards an articulation of Woolf's "common sentence," Potter's film provides us with three areas that require final analysis:

1   The film's narrative engagement with the myth of the impoverished, genius artist (a myth that Woolf works to dismantle in *A Room of One's Own*);

2 Potter's ability to foreground direct audience engagement with Orlando, making the relationship between the audience and Orlando complicit;

3 Potter's ability to use this turn towards the audience as a way to linger on her characters and locations without fetishizing them.

Through these strategies, Potter works to make *Orlando* at once an adaptation of Woolf's novel and an adaptation of *A Room of One's Own*, crafting a cinematic syntax that is deeply feminist and, I argue, uniquely queer.

NICK GREENE: Or, the masculine myth of genius in poverty

Narrative links between Potter's film *Orlando*, Woolf's novel *Orlando*, and Woolf's *A Room of One's Own* may seem obvious; *Orlando* is about someone who, when deemed to be a woman, is forcibly stripped of their physical space. In both Woolf's novel and Potter's film, Orlando's relationship with Nick Greene (a poet Orlando admires) is a more covert moment of narrative cohesion with Woolf's *A Room of One's Own*, one that serves to visualize Woolf's ideas about the links between poverty and creative genius that are at the core of that text.

About a third of the way into Potter's film (a moment in which we still understand Orlando as "male"), Orlando invites Nick Greene to their home for a meal and conversation. Greene, a boorish oaf played brilliantly by Heathcote Williams, has a clear distaste for those born into money and for the material goods (and spaces) to which they have access. After an awkward visit to Orlando's residence, Greene convinces Orlando to pay a quarterly pension in exchange for his thoughts about Orlando's poetry. This payment, however, does not guarantee a positive review. Ever the critic, Greene pens a scathing critique of Orlando's poetry:

Figure 29
Sally Potter directs Heathcote Williams on the set of *Orlando*.

Try as he might, this gracious noble Lord
Who lifts his pen and thinks he then can write
Cannot – for who can write when they are bored?
The mind of leisure only can be trite
This pretty knight who feebly lifts his sword
To make a witless thrust against his doom
Is foiled by what his noble birth affords –
Dogs, dogs, more dogs and far too many rooms.
So fortune smiles on those who own the land
And frowns on trivia from the dabbler's hand.

The poem that Greene sends to Orlando, written by Potter for the film (Mayer 2009, 99), demonstrates that Greene embraces a logic that understands "the great poets [to] have often been poor men" (Woolf, [1929] 2019, 87). Greene, a struggling author who explains his own financial troubles to Orlando over dinner, is clearly critical of the space of the nobles. In Woolf's novel, we read of Greene's own living situation as a contrast to Orlando's. Upon returning to his own home, Greene "found things going on much as he had left them. Mrs Greene, that is to say, was giving birth to a baby in one room; Tom Fletcher was drinking gin in another. Books were tumbled all about the floor; dinner – such as it was – was set on a dressing-table where the children had been making mud pies. But this, Greene felt, was the atmosphere for writing; here he could write and he did" (Woolf, [1928] 2006, 94–5). For Woolf, Greene's criticism is less about a specific work of Orlando's and more about their entire living situation. In both Potter's and Woolf's *Orlando*, Greene believes that life's challenges and interruptions allow a man the chance to craft something of importance. When life is most overwhelming, Greene seems to think, a man can write a masterpiece. When a man has the means to live leisurely, he must be bored.

An understanding of artistic genius as linked to poverty is one of the central targets of Woolf's *A Room of One's Own*. Woolf quotes Sir Arthur Quiller-Couch in his observations that, of most of the "great poetical names of the last hundred years," perhaps one of twelve was "not fairly well to do" ([1929] 2019, 87–8). "It may seem a brutal thing to say," Quiller-Couch writes, "but, as a matter of hard fact, the theory that poetical genius bloweth where it listeth, and equally in poor and rich, holds little truth … The poor poet has not in these days, nor has had for two hundred years a dog's chance" (Woolf [1929] 2019, 88).

The logic that Quiller-Couch (and Woolf and subsequently Potter, by extension) is combatting, in all its awful glorification of poverty, is a complex issue for Nick Greene. In the film, Orlando's first encounter with Greene occurs in Orlando's dining room, an ornate space adorned with silver and wood panelling deserving of any British noble's home-turned-museum. As Greene and Orlando sit at opposite ends of a long dining table, Greene begins their conversation by positioning himself as a direct descendant of "the highest nobility in France." Greene clearly sees value in having aristocratic blood, using his family lineage to justify his presence. "Unfortunately," Greene says, "the Greenes came down in the world and we've done little more than leave our name to the Borough of Greenwich." We see Greene's literal hunger as he laps up the soup that Orlando's valet has brought to the table. Orlando's wealth is made absurd by comparison.

When Greene wants to discuss the basic human needs that he faces, Orlando is uninterested. When Orlando tries to quickly turn the subject to poetry, Greene takes an abrupt turn in tone. "If we are to speak of poetry," he says, "then let us first speak of poets' lives. Do you know how *Hamlet* was written? Written whilst bailiffs were pounding at Shakespeare's door … How can a genius write when he cannot pay the bills?" Greene seems to both espouse the fantasy of poetry blossoming from poverty – after all, he finds himself quite poor and quite the poetic genius – while simultaneously demanding that Orlando provide a quarterly pension of £300, which would allow him "to live for literature alone" (Potter and Woolf 1994, 27). What began as a moment in which we might have identified with Greene in his struggle to acquire the basic necessities of life is transformed into a hypocritical caricature of the poor, noble poet. Through his aggressiveness and, later, his berating of Orlando in verse, the poet has been exposed as a cruel hustler.

The audience's understanding of the quality of Greene and Orlando's poetry poses an additional layer of complexity to their dynamic. As So Mayer points out, the poetry for which Orlando solicits Greene's feedback is "heartfelt," but it "lacks style, wit, and originality" (2009, 99). By comparison, Greene's response to Orlando is painful *because it is clever*. While Orlando's poems may not be cutting in the way that Greene's are, and while the disparities in affluence between these two characters provide a clear visual difference that we may then choose to attach to Greene's "good" and Orlando's "bad" poetry, Greene is clearly the grotesque figure in their encounter. In the moment, we – like Orlando – are put off by Greene and his words. When Orlando's valet asks, in response to the cruel poem, what should be done about Mr Greene's pension, Orlando's response to "pay it quarterly" only makes our empathy for Orlando grow. Yet, although we are meant to side with Orlando in their encounter with Greene, the film also reinforces the accuracy of Greene's critique.

The audience is only given three moments in Potter's *Orlando* in which Orlando's poetry (or reading of poetry) is assigned a value judgment. First, Orlando recites poetry for Queen Elizabeth (played by Quentin Crisp) early in the film; this performance is deemed unsuitable, as Orlando is reading an excerpt of Edmund Spenser's *The Faerie Queene* which describes the death of a queen. In this scene, although the audience is not encountering Orlando's original verse, Potter shows Orlando to be naive in their understanding of poetry. Second, as discussed above, Orlando recites a poem to Nick Greene, which is (justifiably) returned with poetic scorn. Third (and finally), we encounter "a male publisher (who looks like an extremely smart, sharp-suited version of Nick Greene)" (and played by the same actor), who is in a meeting with the now-female Orlando. Mere minutes from the conclusion of the film, the publisher provides Orlando with their first and only moment of praise: "it's really very good," he says. "Written from the heart. I think it will sell. Providing you re-write a little. You know, develop the love interest and give it a happy ending" (Potter and Woolf 1994, 59). This backhanded compliment is not welcomed by Orlando, who looks to the camera knowingly before riding off on a motorcycle with their daughter to visit the home that was taken from them.

Upon first viewing, it may seem that Greene was right: the space of leisure that Greene so despises (or envies, perhaps) is the same space that is taken from Orlando when they become a woman. It takes Orlando becoming disenfranchised, removed from their home, and a parent in the 1990s before they are able to complete a "good" work of literature. Although we do not agree with Greene's method of critiquing Orlando, we understand the truth of the opinion. Further adding to the validity of Greene's critique, Orlando's writing is only deemed "very good" *after* they have lost their home and affluence. In these last moments, we might read Potter's film as an ultimate embrace of the logic that Greene espouses and Woolf combats in *A Room of One's Own*.

This reading, however, neglects a crucial detail: Orlando's gaze. In that brief moment after the "male publisher" tells Orlando that they will need to rewrite, Orlando looks at us knowingly. With their hair pulled back and braided, Orlando's style is what Hollinger and Winterhalter describe as "retro-chic" (2001, 252). While their use of the term is intended as a critique of *Orlando*'s engagement with issues of class, I read this attire differently. To my mind, the retro-chic garments continue the project of situating Orlando transhistorically. As Ferriss and Waites note, Sandy Powell's wardrobe design amplifies the fact that "clothing ... does more than simply mark femininity (or masculinity)" (1999, 112). Powell's garments for Orlando's 1990s look are unique in their relationship to the "problematic of gender-fixing" in so far as Orlando – now female – is dressed markedly masculine. Throughout the film, Orlando's wardrobe makes dramatic shifts based on the gendered expectations of their embodiment in a specific time, but the retro-chic attire of the film's end is an important break from this pattern. Resonating with a 1990s aesthetic while feeling like a riding costume from Britain's past, Orlando is positioned as more in control of themselves and of their time in this encounter with the publisher – who is a Nick Greene stand-in if not literally Nick Greene himself – than they have been previously. It is with this newfound command that Orlando's gaze towards the audience speaks volumes – it is brimming with distrust of, and disdain for, this too-suave publisher whose "commentary about narrative suggests a critique of the Hollywood formula for a successful film," as film scholar Anne Ciecko has argued (1998, 31). Orlando's response to camera, then, is one that is knowingly about literature and film; having lived across gender for nearly four hundred years, Orlando's perpetual naivety has finally gone, even if the agelessness appears to remain. With Orlando's

Figure 30
Orlando and their daughter ride a motorbike to Orlando's old home.

eyes meeting ours, Potter cuts to a close-up of Orlando's "foot starting a motorbike" (Potter and Woolf 1994, 60). Through that edit, I understand the film
to imply that Orlando will not continue pursuing a relationship with the pub-
lisher/Nick Greene. The film will not "develop the love interest and give [us]
a happy ending" and neither will Orlando's manuscript.

As Orlando drives themself and their daughter from this meeting and up
to their lost family estate, the grand topiaries and trees that lined the entrance
way are now covered in white plastic – the home of leisure has been made absurd. Inside, Orlando and her daughter explore the halls of the home, now a
living museum. Orlando, along with a host of visitors, gazes upon a portrait
of themself as a young man. In voiceover, Orlando tells us that they are "no

longer trapped by destiny." "Ever since she let go of the past," the audience is told, "she found her life was beginning." In these moments of voiceover and direct address to the camera, the audience understands their place alongside Orlando – working towards a freedom from the imperialist control that the family estate signifies. In Potter's imagining of *Orlando*, the historical and cultural connotations of gender bind us. It is not that our protagonist needs to become disenfranchised to write well, a myth that Woolf also argues against in *A Room of One's Own*, but that we must find ourselves alive in the present; finding our voices – and embodiment – through our own unique complexity.

BREAKING THE FOURTH WALL: Or, the audience as company

While Potter incorporates elements of Woolf's *A Room of One's Own* in thematic ways through Orlando's relationship with Greene, she also works to craft a unique cinematic grammar, embracing Woolf's call for women to create a "common sentence." One tool that Potter employs is Orlando's often-discussed fourth wall breaks, challenging Hollywood conventions in a film that features an otherwise third-person structure. The challenges to these conventions are made plain in the opening scene of the film, which revels in the complexity of Orlando's gaze and subjectivity.

In wide shot, the film opens with its titular character under an oak tree. Orlando walks from side to side, memorizing poetry under the tree. As Orlando paces, the camera moves at the same speed. As Orlando walks right, the camera moves left, keeping Orlando in frame while highlighting the artificiality of camera movement. When Orlando pauses, the camera remains still. In voiceover, we hear Tilda Swinton explain that "there can be no doubt about his sex – despite the feminine appearance that every young man of the time aspires to. And there can be no doubt about his upbringing. Good food, education, a nanny, loneliness and isolation." Orlando pauses at this point, walking to the tree and sitting with their back resting on the tree's trunk. This first shot, which lasts approximately forty-five seconds, introduces us to the slow, observant pacing of Potter's film.

This first shot also helps us understand the positioning of the gaze(s) present in the film. As film scholar So Mayer argues, "there are two gazes occurring in the opening of *Orlando*: the first is the camera's, which is unattributed despite the swaying shot being quite ostentatious; the second is Orlando's" (2009, 50). This dual gaze becomes obvious when, in the next shot, we hear Swinton's voiceover continue: "and because this is England, Orlando would therefore seem destined to have his portrait on the wall and his name in the history books. But when he —" the onscreen version of Orlando then interrupts their own voiceover, turning directly towards camera and engaging with us. "That is, I," they say. Averting their gaze again, the voiceover continues: when they "came into the world, he was looking for something else. Though heir to a name which meant power, land and property, surely when Orlando was born it wasn't privilege he sought, but company." In accord with Mayer's argument, there is a clear difference here in point of view between the shots that appear to be from a detached third-person perspective and the ones in which we are directly acknowledged by Orlando.

Orlando's address to the camera, however, complicates an understanding of there being a simple divide in gaze between us and Orlando. Pulling from a Brechtian tradition in which "direct address to the camera/audience … distances the audience" from the ability to remain passive, we are invited to become involved "in the act of constructing meaning along with the character and the film's narrative" (Ferriss and Waites 1999, 111). Because Orlando is able to interrupt a third-person gaze and because the camera is directly tied to Orlando's movement even when in third person, we must assume that Orlando is always conscious of the camera's gaze and, therefore, we are encouraged to question moments of third-person representation. This ultimately leads to an undermining of the third person altogether; this undoing of a familiar mode of cinematic representation begins in these first moments and continues throughout the entirety of the film.

These initial moments introduce us to Orlando, of course, but they also introduce us to the "common sentence" that the film will be drawing from and modifying. The cinematic grammar that the film is working to establish (the "common sentence" in Woolf's terminology) employs the camera and direct address to allow the audience to exist somewhere between first and third person, between the biographer and the autobiographer, between director and actor. To a certain extent, this approach recalls the work of French New Wave filmmakers of the 1960s and 1970s who were similarly invested in an equally Brechtian approach. Working to complicate the space between audience and image as an attack on a "Tradition of Quality," these New Wave works greeted their audiences with a gritty realism that saw fourth wall breaks amidst a host of other practices to encourage distanciation. While we might consider the political aims of the French New Wave as a part of the "common sentence" that Potter is working with, her film manages to envelop us inside of Orlando's consciousness, relying heavily on the aesthetic beauty of costume drama, rather than encouraging us to understand our natural position outside of the film's diegesis. From the very first moments of her film, Potter invites us to be complicit in Orlando's journey, to be the company that Orlando seeks, but also to *be* Orlando in the way that an autobiography allows us to *be* the person writing. In so doing, Potter mixes our own gaze and Orlando's in a way that encourages an erosion in our understanding of that difference.

To my mind, Virginia Woolf's assertion that "any great [female] figure of the past ... is an inheritor as well as an originator, and has come into existence because women have come to have the habit of writing naturally" ([1929] 2019, 89) is particularly important in understanding this fluidity in point of view. Perhaps most obviously, adaptation requires the inheritance of a work and, with *Orlando*, Potter is inheriting directly from Woolf. In Woolf's *Orlando*, which foregrounds cheeky, formal play with the generic conventions and formulas of the "biography," the reader is constantly reminded of the process of writing through the insertion of the biographer's voice. For example, the second chapter of Woolf's text begins: "The biographer is now faced with a difficulty which it is better perhaps to confess than to gloss over. Up to this point in telling the story of Orlando's life, documents, both private and historical, have made it possible to fulfil the first duty of a biographer, which is to plod, without looking to right or left, in the indelible foot-prints of truth; unenticed by flowers; regardless of shade; on and on methodically till we fall plump into the grave and write *finis* on the tombstone above our heads" (Woolf [1928] 2006, 65). In these pseudo-methodological passages, we are reminded of the formal process of writing, but also of the interpretive powers of the one holding the pen. By writing that the biographer is merely a carrier of "the indelible foot-prints of truth," Woolf makes us aware of how false that statement is. In crafting such deeply unnatural, pompous prose, Woolf positions the (assumedly masculine) role of "the biographer" as an outsider. The joy of Woolf's text, in my reading, stems from the moments in Orlando's life that "the biographer" finds so impossible to articulate "methodically." The moments when the biographer is forced to stop, enticed by flowers and spaces and bodies – in other words, when the methodological form of the biography breaks down – the novel becomes all the more queer.

In Potter's cinematic adaptation, the character of "the biographer" is removed; there is no third party working to craft the narrative of Orlando's life. While we may be inclined to understand the omission of "the biographer" as a way for Orlando to tell their own queer story, Orlando's constant gaze at the camera/us complicates our own relationship to the form of the film. Productively problematizing this relationship between first- and third-person perspective in the film, Suzanne Ferriss and Kathleen Waites note that "the voice-over presents a third person point of view at odds with the narrative frame established by the film, which is, by its very nature, a third person point of view as well. The first person direct address to the camera disrupts both. In addition, while both the frame of the film and the direct address are contemporaneous with the viewer's experience of the film in the present, the voice-over is retrospective, recounting events that have occurred in the past" (1999, 111). Potter's audience is faced with an unfamiliar combination of narrative components that signal both third- and first-person perspective, muddying the audience's ability to cleanly define the point of view in these moments.

While this poses a unique problem for understanding *Orlando*'s perspective in conventional cinematic terms, which would situate the film as somehow about and authored by our character, it is helpful to think of Potter's film in league with histories of portrait painting. Describing the relationship between portrait painter and sitter, George Keyes, the former curator of the Detroit Institute of the Arts, explains that "by its nature, portraiture involves a certain kind of collaboration … The quest for likeness as a collaborative enterprise could, in a certain sense, also be understood as conspiratorial … Does the artist idealize, fantasize, or, conversely, is he or she allowed varying degrees of candor as a means of capturing the individuality of the sitter as measured by the subject's unique physiognomy, blemishes and all?" (2009, 4). These, I think, are fascinating questions for understanding our own relationship to Orlando.

In the first moments of the film, for example, when we see Orlando positioned beneath the oak tree, we might first understand Orlando as simply sitting and we are simply watching them – the typical film voyeur. They have been pacing, they take a seat beneath the tree, and we then cut to a close-up of them leaning against the tree's trunk. However, when Orlando turns towards the camera to interrupt their own voiceover, breaking the fourth wall, Orlando ruptures our sense of the third-person point of view of the scene. As Orlando self-consciously re-averts their gaze, our understanding of their relationship to the space of the oak tree, to Potter's camera, and to us as the audience has now changed dramatically. As film scholar Cristina Degli-Esposti argues, "Potter uses the technique of baroque portraiture" to focus "on the optical encounter between us and the character, who becomes, for the duration of the eye contact, part of our world and vice versa" (1996, 78). In this transcendent relationship between Orlando and *Orlando*'s audience, the film makes us aware of our status as confidant and co-conspirator and also high-lights the artificiality of the more conventionally third-person perspective that exists throughout the bulk of the film. Taking it a step further than Degli-Esposti, I argue that, once we know that Orlando "sees" us under the oak tree, we are able to understand all third-person moments throughout the film as a form of posing. Thus, we become complicit even in the moments in which we are not acknowledged by Orlando. To my mind, the divide between our world and Orlando's is encouraged to erode completely.

This way of understanding the relationship between Orlando and the film's audience is in accord with George Piggford's understanding of "female camp," in which he argues that the "female androgyne ... suggests that the biological sex of the performer is an important aspect of the attempt to un-settle notions of gender, especially in cultures in which the male is regarded as the norm. These female/androgynous figures do not simply dress as men; rather, they are women who dress, perform, write, appear as gendered iden-tities that might be placed in a range between masculine and feminine. These women employ a camp sensibility – a code of appearance and behavior that mocks and ironizes gender norms – in order to undermine the gender as-sumptions of their specific cultures" (1997, 40). When Swinton looks to us as Orlando, we know that we are in on – and an important element of – *Orlando*'s critique of gender because we see the discrepancy between Swinton's assumed/assigned gender and that of Orlando at the beginning of the film. As discussed in the first chapter of this book, the break between Swinton's own star image and the world of the film becomes an important avenue by which Potter in-vites us into a knowing relationship with Orlando.

Through this relationship, moments under the oak tree that would have otherwise read as third-person perspective end up feeling like we are sitting next to Orlando with a brush as they pose for the portrait we are painting of them. This understanding of the stillness of these moments as aligned with the conceptual framework of painting is in accord with theorist Jackie Stacey's argument that the film functions around a series of composed still life paintings (2015, 260). I would add that, through its formal experimentation, the audience is encouraged to imagine themselves there; we are in it with Orlando/Swinton and, through Orlando's voiceover and fourth wall breaks, we are encouraged to think of ourselves as a fundamental part of the story. As a result, Potter takes Woolf's "biography" into the realm of a collaborative *autobiography*. By desaturating her film of "the biographer's" methodological passages, Potter allows us to embrace Orlando's journey as a surprisingly natural one. The biographer's difficulty explaining Orlando's longevity and change of sex, which are expressed in extended prose in Woolf's novel, pose no problem for Potter's lens. Instead, Potter's audience is presented with a free flowing, morphing journey *alongside* (rather than *about*) Orlando. The formal shifts from first to third person – sometimes in the same shot – act as a mirror of the fluidity that Orlando experiences with regard to their own body and sense of self.

This oscillating experience of point of view, to my mind, is a far more "natural" way of approaching subjectivity than we are used to in mainstream Hollywood film viewing. As cinema goers, most audiences have come to expect third-person point of view in film, but this simply is not the way we encounter the outside world. In our everyday experience of being with one another, we constantly see through our own eyes while transporting ourselves into the eyes of others – empathizing, imagining, and seeing how our companions, colleagues, and friends experience the world by way of our mind's eye. By blending first-person and third-person point of view, Potter undermines the impulse to engage with *Orlando* as a detached voyeur. In so doing, Potter allows us to move between seeing Orlando with our own eyes and seeing Orlando as we imagine Orlando sees themself. This constant fluctuation in perspective, rooted in our empathy for Orlando, allows us the chance to be the thing that Orlando desires most – their company and companion.

Throughout Potter's film, the audience sees Orlando's desire for diegetic company consistently rebuked or denied. Sasha abandons Orlando. Nick

Greene betrays Orlando's admiration, ridiculing and mocking them. The Khan (played by Lothaire Bluteau) asks Orlando to take up arms. After Orlando's dramatic change in sex, they are informed by a drawing room full of "wits and poets" that "the intellect is a solitary place and therefore quite unsuitable a terrain for females who must discover their natures through the guidance of a father or husband." The Archduke Harry – now that Orlando is a woman (what a "charming" surprise!) – expresses a desire to marry them but does not seek to know them intellectually. Thus, every opportunity for companionship afforded to Orlando before their relationship with Shelmerdine (played by Billy Zane) ends in a desire to possess something *of* Orlando(s), whether their property, money, or body. When Shelmerdine rides away from Orlando to "fight for the future," every person to whom Orlando has wished to give of themself has ultimately refused them.

The camera's gaze, on the other hand, is a longing one, a loving one, a gentle and reciprocal one. We want nothing of Orlando except for the company they/we crave. A desire to find company in the images on screen, after all, is one of the reasons why audiences go to the movies.[3] Yet, this is dramatically different from the way we have come to understand the language of film. As film theorist Laura Mulvey describes in her germinal essay "Visual Pleasure and Narrative Cinema," "the mass of mainstream film[s] … portray a hermetically sealed world which unwinds magically, indifferent to the presence of the audience, producing for them a sense of separation and playing on their voyeuristic phantasy" (1988, 60). The conventional way of approaching cinema encourages us to see films as self-sealing and fully enclosed worlds, something for us to view and take pleasure in from afar. Potter's approach, on the other hand, breaks with Mulvey's way of describing the "hermetically sealed world" of most mainstream films. In Potter's hands, the camera (and the audience, by extension) is the companion that Orlando craves.

AGAINST FETISHIZATION: Or, a longing that doesn't do violence

One of the joys of *Orlando* is certainly the pleasure of looking. With its slow pacing and beautifully composed images, Potter invites us to take our time devouring the colours, lights, frozen rivers, exotic landscapes, and beautiful bodies that are on display in the film. Orlando's ownership over (or, at the very least, cognizance of) the images being produced of them, however, allows Potter to linger on images of Orlando's body while simultaneously undermining the audience's ability to fetishize them.

In "Visual Pleasure and Narrative Cinema," Mulvey writes of the way in which conventional Hollywood cinema positions the "pleasure in looking" as "split between active/male and passive/female" (1988, 61). Mulvey notes that the "cult of the female star" is indebted to a "fetishistic scopophilia," which "turns the represented figure itself into something satisfying in itself" (1988, 64). In Mulvey's argument, we do violence to the women on screen by devaluing them and turning them into fetish objects, and this is done in large part through the process of pleasurable looking. With prose that echoes the sentiment of Woolf's *A Room of One's Own*, Mulvey writes that "there is no way in which we can produce an alternative out of the blue, but we can begin to make a break by examining patriarchy with the tools it provides" (1988, 58). Like Woolf, Mulvey longs for another language, another "common sentence" (a visual one, in this case) with which women can take ownership over their narratives and representation.

Orlando is a particularly interesting film with regard to Mulvey's argument, I believe, because we *could* accuse it of encouraging fetishistic scopophilia. For all of the temporal leaps that are a crucial part of Woolf's text and Potter's film, Potter's script does rely on the classical narrative structure of mainstream film. Providing her audience with a clear protagonist, a host of forces working against them, and a three-act structure, Potter fools us into believing this film will operate like any other. Furthermore, as the film has found new audiences over the course of the last twenty years, Tilda Swinton's ever growing star persona could be read as an example of our modern "cult of the female star." Certainly, Swinton's body is placed on display throughout *Orlando* – from adoring close-ups to a full-frontal nude reveal. And yet, as Cristina Degli-Esposti argues, *Orlando* provides a complex web of pleasures (for both Orlando and the *Orlando*'s audience). "When looking back," Degli-Esposti writes, "Orlando shares visual pleasure with the viewer. When looking into the camera, Orlando directs his/her pleasure to an invisible audience of which he/she is constantly aware" (1996, 83). In so doing, the film functions as a part of the conversation about and a complication to Mulvey's arguments. If we do carry through the logic outlined in "Visual Pleasure" and understand *Orlando* to be promoting a scopophilic response that makes Swinton's body an object for our consumption, we hit a snag. Why does the film – and the full-frontal nude scene, in particular – pose such mental roadblocks for heterosexual, cisgender individuals who are attuned to the process of fetishization, even if they are not able to name it as such?

I argue that, in large part, the answer lies in the ways in which the film is a caring collaboration: a collaboration between director and actor as well as one between character and audience. As mundane as that may seem, a true, careful, caring collaboration is something that we see far too infrequently in a film production context (read: Hollywood) that understands the value of moving images solely in terms of their status as economic product. Potter's audience faces an uphill battle in an attempt to sexualize them beyond their own desire for us to do so for a host of reasons. First, because *we* are Orlando's companion through Potter's structural mixing of third- and first-person point of view. Second, because Orlando maintains control over their narrative and image through direct address and voiceover. And, third, because we see Orlando as they see themselves.

Audience members who approach the film by mapping a fetishistic gaze onto the bodies on screen – insofar as that is our dominant training as cinemagoers – find a mirror in the Archduke Harry (played by John Wood). When the Archduke learns that Orlando is now the "Lady" Orlando, his response is to celebrate Orlando's new status as woman (and thereby, an object) by exclaiming, "and to think we could have been so *charmingly* mislead!" In Harry's statement, we see an insistence on binary gender. If Orlando is a woman now, Orlando has always been a woman. They were able to pose as a man for so long – how alluring! In response, the Archduke proposes marriage – what else is an eligible bachelor to do? After all, he has always seen them as the "pink, the pearl and the pinnacle of [their] sex." And what a feminizing sentiment that is! For the Archduke, Orlando's unhesitating rejection of his marriage proposal is baffling. "You are refusing me?" he asks. "Do you realize what you are turning down? ... You will die a spinster. Dispossessed and alone." Confusion quickly turns to anger – if the Archduke cannot have the "Lady" Orlando, what is the point of Orlando's being at all? The Archduke's troubling line of thought, here, is strikingly similar to those audience members who attempt to map a learned fetishistic scopophilic gaze onto Potter's *Orlando*. "If I cannot engage with this film in the way that I know," this thought pattern leads, "then why engage at all?" Orlando's snarky response to the Archduke's cruel insult – simply "Spinster! Alone!" – is the perfect queer comeback. Throwing the Archduke's words back in his face, Orlando demands that there must be a way to exist outside of the dominant system of representation.

When Orlando returns to their lost estate with their daughter in the final moments of the film, they pause in front of a portrait of themselves. Outlined in the first voiceover of the film, the cycle of Orlando's representation is complete: Orlando was, in fact, "destined to have his portrait on the wall." Is this the portrait we have been painting throughout the film? Sitting under the oak tree again, the film comes to a close. A shiny, gold angel (played by Jimmy Somerville, who played Queen Elizabeth's soprano at the beginning of the film) sings above Orlando and their daughter: "In this moment of unity / I'm feeling only an ecstasy / To be here, to be now / At last I am free / Yes – at last, at last / To be free of the past." As Orlando's daughter runs around the field playing with a video recorder, she approaches a now teary-eyed Orlando. Through the daughter's camera, we see Orlando as they look straight into the

Figure 31
A glittering angel (played by Jimmy Somerville) sings above Orlando and
their daughter.

lens. "Why are you sad?" the child asks. "I'm not. I'm happy," Orlando replies.
This "happiness" has been read by scholars Karen Hollinger and Teresa Winterhalter as allowing Orlando and their daughter to escape into the "idyllic
green woman's world" of nature that exists for them under the oak tree (1994,
11). To my mind, however, this interpretation negates the deep sense of mourn-
ing and loss that accompanies Orlando's "happiness" in the concluding moments of the film.

From the first moment that we see that Orlando is pregnant, their child is
tied up with what Jane Maree Maher has described as a "conflict" between the
pregnant woman and her body. This conflict is made literal in the only moment where we see Orlando's pregnant body; as they traverse a world war–
style battlefield, stumbling between explosions, it is clear that their "pregnancy

weighs her down and makes it hard for her to move forward" in both literal and symbolic terms (Maher 2007, 24). Although the battlefield also serves to launch the audience into a new stage of Orlando's life – one of acceptance and growth, perhaps – we are still generations away from utopia.

So Mayer argues that, in the film's final moments under the oak tree, there is a suggestion "that the daughter has been, all along, the author of a film portrait of her mother." In their reading of this scene, Mayer argues that "it is this daughter whom Orlando has been addressing when she speaks to camera, so she is also the audience born within and into the film, and given the tools to leave the cinema and reinvent art" (2009, 103). While I do not read this moment in quite the same way as Mayer – I would much prefer to leave the strange potential of the fourth wall breaking open for the viewer's insertion of themselves – it is clear to me that the filmmaker, here articulated with an exploratory enthusiasm that comes naturally to children, is certainly an "inheritor" in the sense that Woolf describes in A Room of One's Own. Orlando's daughter/Potter is taking up the means of production with a newly emergent "common sentence." In so doing, this allows the next generation to take up Potter's cinematic "sentence," revealing Orlando's child to be our parent as much as she is us.

As audiences watch Orlando now, decades after its release, generational rereading queers the already multifaceted implications of Orlando's daughter until the relationship between Orlando and their child becomes a supernova. In her ability to hold the camera aimed at her writerly mother, the child in the grass becomes Potter and Orlando becomes a projection of Woolf. Yet, in so far as Potter's adaptation visualizes Woolf's "common sentence," Potter invites us – through the image of the daughter – to take up cameras of our own, practising and modifying the cinematic language we now share. And, thus, the daughter is as much us as she is Potter. But age and relationships are fraught for Orlando; if we are inheriting Potter's "common sentence" through the film Orlando, then Potter is Orlando as much as she is Orlando's daughter. In all of this projection, it is clear to me that Woolf and Potter are co-conspirators in the exploding of normative subjectivity. As their audience, we become the children of Woolf and Potter's union, and they are the queer children of their own creating, the embodiment of Woolf's understanding that female writers are both "inheritor[s] as well as … originator[s]" (Woolf [1929] 2019, 89). Motherhood and childhood merge and morph. Generational boundaries are dissolved in pursuit of other forms of intellectual connection.

This generational rereading has only made Potter's film queerer over time. Originally scorned for the elimination of lesbian relationships, Potter instead managed to craft a work that speaks to our current queer world, a moment which continues to see (and embrace) complications to binary understandings of gender. There are certainly arguments to be made that by sidelining Orlando's same-sex encounters, Potter may have been working to imagine a feminist version of a lesbian feminist text. But the film's children – that is, those of us who read into the film with the same fervour with which Orlando speaks to us – have revelled in the queerness that we so clearly see in it. This is not a queerness of identity politics. It is not a queerness centred in sex. It is a queerness that sees itself as in a constant process of becoming. It is queerness that sees categorical and binary logic as a detriment to our complex selves. It is a queerness that understands time as far from linear. As we pursue new ways of understanding our being, I am convinced that Sally Potter's *Orlando* will continue to allow viewers opportunities to modify our mothers' "common sentences" in ever morphing, queer ways.

Notes

Introduction

1 The film was also to be the inspiration point for the 2020 Met Gala (Borrelli-Persson 2020, Phelps 2019).

2 This is an issue that Potter has expressed frustrations with for decades. In 2017, Potter addressed the shifting nature of the issue in an interview with Guy Lodge for the *Guardian*. In that interview, she explains: "I'm completely proud of the word [feminist]. The feminist movement is one of the most vibrant, extraordinary political movements of the 20th century, and now there's a younger generation who's taken it up again with great joy and pleasure, and that's wonderful to see. But I object to the way it's used as a prefix to my work, to ghettoise it, often as part of a criticism rather than an appreciation. I just want to occupy a free space without a prefix. Because what does it mean? I have to ask someone, what exactly do you mean by that term and what is it adding to anyone's understanding who might go and see the film?" (Lodge 2017).

3 Rich points to films like *My Own Private Idaho* (Gus Van Sant, 1991) and *The Living End* (Gregg Araki, 1992) as exemplary of these gay male voices and films. For film theorist Glyn Davis's argument as to why and how we might still consider *Orlando* to be a part of the New Queer Cinema, see Davis (2016, 167–9).

4 For lesbian feminist readings of Woolf (and specifically of *Orlando*), see Meese (1992) and Knopp (1988).

5 Those four films include: *The Tango Lesson* (1997), *The Man Who Cried* (2000), *Yes* (2004), and *The Party* (2017), although *The Party* does feature a lesbian couple as two of its central characters.

6 Specifically, I have embraced the methodological model provided by Alexander Doty's chapter "Everyone's Here for Love: Bisexuality and *Gentlemen Prefer Blondes*" in his book *Flaming Classics* (2010). In this chapter, Doty reads Marilyn Monroe and Jane Russell's relationship in *Gentlemen Prefer Blondes* (Howard Hawks, 1953) as a subtly but centrally bisexual one.

Chapter One

1 Caroline Evans and Lorraine Gamman's essay "Reviewing Queer Viewing" is helpful in thinking about the ways one might apply the term "genderfuck" to film and reception (2004).

2 For more on the music in *Orlando*, see Martin (2011).

3 In his final autobiography, *The Last Word* (published posthumously and compiled from audio recordings that Phillip Ward made with Crisp late in life), Crisp explains that "My daydream as a child was of growing up to be a very worldly, beautiful woman … At the age of ninety, it has finally been explained to me that I am not really a homosexual, I'm transgender. I now accept that … I don't see myself as a man though, of course, I know I'm not physically a woman" (2017, 4–5). As is described in *The Last Word*, Crisp experienced firsthand the changes in identity and categorization that shifts in language allow.

4 Although Crisp articulated himself as a "transgender woman" in his last autobiography, as far as I understand, Crisp used he/him/his pronouns up until his death. For that reason, when necessary, I use "he" to refer to Crisp in this chapter.

5   I find Suzanne Ferriss and Kathleen Waites's notes about the onscreen
     relationship between Swinton's Orlando and Crisp's Queen Elizabeth I
     to be particularly helpful in conceptualizing their potential queer cou-
     pling: "another occasion finds Orlando, the favored 'son' of Elizabeth
     and recipient of properties on the condition that he never 'grow old,'
     alone in his bed pondering the eccentric queen, her whims and his own
     fortune, before looking sideways at the camera and observing: 'A very
     interesting person.' The scene highlights both the construction of the
     narrative and of sexuality, for the male Orlando, [who] is played by a
     female actress, Tilda Swinton, addresses the female queen, played by
     a male homosexual. Orlando's intrusion, coupled with our knowledge
     of the actors' gender switching, not only breaks the illusion of narrative
     wholeness but forces us to recognize that the film itself is an illusion"
     (1999, 111).
6   For more on Swinton's performance of "flat affect," see Stacey (2015).
7   In Woolf's Orlando, this romance lasts for a very clearly demarcated
     "six months and half" ([1928] 2006, 32).
8   A peruke was a style of wig popular in England from the seventeenth
     through the nineteenth century.
9   Like Tilda Swinton and Quentin Crisp, Lothaire Bluteau's star image is
     one that has been invested in LGBTQ+ narratives, especially in the years
     following Orlando's release. Specifically, see Le Confessionnal (Robert
     Lepage, 1995) and Bent (Sean Mathias, 1997). For a queer reading of
     Le Confessionnal, see Dickinson (2007).
10 Sandy Powell's stunning work on Sally Potter's Orlando received an
     Academy Award nomination for Best Costume Design. Orlando's Ben
     van Os and Jan Roelfs also received an Academy Award nomination
     for Best Production Design.
11 Both Potter's and Woolf's versions of Orlando feature a playful rebuke
     of the real historical figures Alexander Pope, Jonathan Swift, and
     Joseph Addison.

12 Hollinger and Winterhalter argue that Potter's film understands "oppression via gender [to have] ended" in its search for a genderless ideal (2001, 249). This, in their argument, stands counter to Woolf's understanding that oppression based on gender is/was very much alive.

13 Elizabeth Freeman is building upon Jack Halberstam's note that understanding "queer time" requires us to "think about queerness as an outcome of strange temporalities, imaginative life schedules, and eccentric economic practices" that exist "in opposition to the institutions of family, heterosexuality, and reproduction." In so doing, Halberstam argues, "we detach queerness from sexual identity" (2005, 1).

Chapter Two

1 Depending on the source, the timeline from development to completion for *Orlando* ranges from about seven years to about ten years. Based on the first notes about the possibility of adapting *Orlando* in Sally Potter's SP-ARK, my understanding of the development-to-distribution timeline for *Orlando* spans from 1984 to 1993.

2 The film was produced as a Russian-French-Dutch-American-Italian-British coproduction.

3 See Reviron-Piégay (2009) as well as Hollinger and Winterhalter (2001).

4 For more on adaptation theory see Hutcheon (2014). For an introduction to adaptation theory's application in film studies, see Andrew (1984).

5 So Mayer notes that the relationship with Nell is "omitted from all three drafts of Potter's screenplay" (Mayer 2008, 42). In my research, this is not the case, although Mayer cites unpublished screenplay drafts housed at the British Film Institute rather than those housed in SP-ARK's online archive.

6 For slightly different wording, see Woolf ([1928] 2006, 217).

7 See Woolf ([1928] 2006, 218); Potter (1988c, SPA0000804).

8 On the cover page of the draft, the revision is marked as being current as of May 1990. Midway through the draft, however, SP-ARK has the draft dated simply as "1989."

Chapter Three

1 Other scholars have productively linked *Orlando* and *A Room of One's Own*, but most often with regard to Woolf's argument that great minds are "androgynous." Although I disagree with some components of her reading of the film, Catherine Craft-Fairchild's essay (2001) is instructive in this respect.

2 Woolf uses Jane Austen as an example of a female author who seems able to escape this. Instead, Woolf understands Austen to have "looked at [a man's sentence] and laughed at it and devised a perfectly natural, shapely sentence proper for her own use and never departed from it" ([1929] 2019, 63).

3 The film and media studies subdiscipline of reception theory (beginning with the Stuart Hall's article "Encoding/Decoding" [1984]) has illuminated and theorized the ways that people form connections with the bodies they encounter on screen.

References

Andrew, James Dudley. 1984. *Concepts in Film Theory*. Oxford: Oxford University Press.

Baldanza, Frank. 1955. "Orlando and the Sackvilles." PMLA 70, no. 1 (March): 274–9.

Bazin, André. [1949] 2003. "Death Every Afternoon." In *Rights of Realism: Essays on Corporeal Cinema*, edited by Ivonne Margulies, 27–31. Durham: Duke University Press.

Borrelli-Persson, Laird. 2020. "Nearly Three Decades Later, Sally Potter's 'Orlando' Is More Topical Than Ever." *Vogue*, 2 November 2020. https://www.vogue.com/article/sally-potter-s-1992-orlando-movie-with-tilda-swinton-stands-the-test-of-time.

Canby, Vincent. 1993. "Review/Film Festival; Witty, Pretty, Bold, A Real She-Man." *New York Times*, 19 March 1993.

Ciecko, Anne. 1998. "Transgender, Transgenre, and the Transnational: Sally Potter's *Orlando*." *Velvet Light Trap*, no. 11 (Spring): 19–34.

Clay & Diamonds. n.d. "It's All about the &." https://www.clayanddiamonds.org/.

– n.d. "Orlando: The Queer Element." https://www.clayanddiamonds.org/tour.

Corliss, Richard, and Carrie Ross Welch. 1993. "A Film of One's Own." *Time Magazine* 141, no. 23, 7 June 1993.

Craft-Fairchild, Catherine. 2001. "'Same Person ... Just a Different Sex':
Sally Potter's Construction of Gender in *Orlando*." *Woolf Studies Annual*
7: 23–48.

Crisp, Quentin. 2000. *The Naked Civil Servant; How to Become a Virgin;
Resident Alien*. New York: Quality Paperback Book Club.

– 2017. *The Last Word: An Autobiography*. Edited by Laurence Watts and
Phillip Ward. San Diego, CA: MB Books.

Davies, Caroline. 2021. "Part of River Thames Freezes amid Sub-Zero Temperatures." *Guardian*, 12 February 2021. https://www.theguardian.com/
uk-news/2021/feb/12/part-of-river-thames-freezes-amid-sub-zero-
temperatures.

Davis, Glyn. 2016. "Queens and Queenliness: Quentin Crisp as *Orlando*'s
Elizabeth I" in *The British Monarchy on Screen*. Mandy Merck (ed.).
Manchester University Press: 155–78.

Degli-Esposti, Cristina. 1996. "Sally Potter's *Orlando* and the Neo-Baroque
Scopic Regime." *Cinema Journal* 36, no. 1 (Autumn): 75–93.

Demory, Pamela. 2019. *Queer/Adaptation: A Collection of Critical Essays*.
Cham: Springer International Publishing.

Dickinson, Peter. 2007. *Screening Gender, Framing GENRE: Canadian Literature into Film*. University of Toronto Press.

Doty, Alexander. 2010. *Flaming Classics: Queering the Film Canon*. New
York: Routledge.

Dyer, Richard. 1986. *Stars*. London: BFI Publishing.

– 2004. *Heavenly Bodies: Film Stars and Society*. 2nd ed. Routledge.

Evans, Caroline, and Lorraine Gamman. 2004. "Reviewing Queer Viewing."
In *Queer Cinema: The Film Reader*, edited by Harry M. Benshoff and Sean
Griffin, 209–24. New York: Routledge.

Ferriss, Suzanne, and Kathleen Waites. 1999. "The Postmodern Sensibility
in Sally Potter's *Orlando*." *Literature/Film Quarterly* 27, no. 2: 110–15.

Florence, Penny. 1993. "A Conversation with Sally Potter." *Screen* 34, no. 3
(October): 275–84.

Fowler, Catherine. 2009. *Sally Potter*. Urbana: University of Illinois Press.

Freeman, Elizabeth. 2010. *Time Binds: Queer Temporalities, Queer Histories*. Durham: Duke University Press.

Halberstam, Jack. *In a Queer Time & Place: Transgender Bodies, Subcultural Lives*. New York University Press, 2005.

Halberstam, Jack, and Collier Schorr. 2019. "*Untitled (Casil) (2015–2018)*." *Aperture Magazine* 235: 56–65.

Hall, Stuart. 1980. "Encoding/Decoding." In *Culture, Media, Language*, edited by Stuart Hall, Dorothy Hobson, Andrew Lowe, and Paul Willis, 128–38. London: Hutchinson.

Hankins, Leslie K. 1995. "Redirections: Challenging the Class Axe and Lesbian Erasure in Potter's *Orlando*." In *Re: Beading, Re: Writing, Re: Teaching Virginia Woolf: Selected Papers from the Fourth Annual Conference on Virginia Woolf*, edited by Eileen Barrett and Patricia Cramer, 168–84. Pace University Press.

Hollinger, Karen, and Teresa Winterhalter. 2001. "Orlando's Sister, Or Sally Potter Does Virginia Woolf in a Voice of Her Own." *Style* 35, no. 2: 237–56.

Hutcheon, Linda. 2014. *Theory of Adaptation*. Taylor and Francis.

James, Caryn. 1993. "FILM VIEW; *Orlando*, Like Its Hero(ine), Is One for the Ages." *New York Times*. 6 June 1993.

Kao, Vivian. 2015. "Adapting Heritage: Reading the Writerly Text in 'Orlando.'" *Literature/Film Quarterly* 43, no. 4: 276–90.

Kennedy, Dominic. 1997. "'Stately Homo' Backs Calls to Abort Gay Babies." *London Times*, 17 (February): 7.

Keyes, George. 2009. "Portraiture – Mirror or Mask?" *Bulletin of the Detroit Institute of Arts* 83, no. 1–4: 4–11.

Kingsley, Erin M. 2014. "Bloodless Birth: Reproduction and the Masculine Mind in Virginia Woolf's *A Room of One's Own*." *Virginia Woolf Miscellany*, no. 86 (Fall): 39–41.

Knopp, Sherron E. 1988. "'If I Saw You Would You Kiss Me?': Sapphism and the Subversiveness of Virginia Woolf's *Orlando*." PMLA 103, no. 1: 24–34.

Lodge, Guy. 2017. "Sally Potter: 'There's Nothing Like Hearing a Whole Place Vibrate with Laughter.'" *Guardian*, 8 October 2017. https://www.theguardian.com/film/2017/oct/08/sally-potter-interview-the-party.

Maher, Jane Maree. 2007. "Prone to Pregnancy: Orlando, Virginia Woolf and Sally Potter Represent the Gestating Body." *Journal of Medical Humanities* 28: 19–30.

Marcus, Jane. 1994. "A Tale of Two Cultures." *Women's Review of Book* 11, no. 4 (January): 11–13.

Martin, Ruth Lee. 2011. "Framing Ambiguity and Desire through Musical Means in Sally Potter's Film *Orlando*." *Music, Sound & the Moving Image* 5, no. 1 (Spring): 25–37.

Mayer, So. 2008. "The Mirror Didn't Crack: Costume Drama & Gothic Horror in Sally Potter's *Orlando*." *Literature/Film Quarterly* 36, no. 1: 39–44.

– 2009. *The Cinema of Sally Potter: a Politics of Love*. London: Wallflower Press, 2009.

McEvoy Foundation for the Arts. 2020. "Exhibition: Orlando." 21 August 2020. https://www.mcevoyarts.org/exhibition/orlando/.

Meese, Elizabeth. 1992. "When Virginia Looked at Vita, What Did She See; Or, Lesbian: Feminist: Woman – What's the Differ(e/a)nce?" *Feminist Studies* 18, no. 1: 99–117.

Mulvey, Laura. 1988. "Visual Pleasure and Narrative Cinema." In *Feminism and Film Theory*, edited by Constance Penley, 57–68. New York: Routledge.

Natharius, David, and Bethany A. Dobkin. 2002. "Feminist Visions of Transformation in *The Ballad of Little Jo*, *The Piano*, and *Orlando*." *Women and Language* 25, no. 1: 9–17.

National Trust. 2015. "Vita Sackville-West and Knole." *National Trust*, 9 June 2015. https://www.nationaltrust.org.uk/knole/features/vita-sackville-west-and-knole.

Nicolson, Nigel. [1973] 1998. *Portrait of a Marriage*. Chicago, IL: The University of Chicago Press: 202–3.

Sony Pictures Classics. n.d. "ORLANDO: Press Kit." https://www.sonyclassics.com/orlando/orlando_presskit.pdf.

Pener, Degen. 1993. "EGOS & IDS; Revealed as an Actress." *New York Times*, 6 June 1993.

Phelps, Nicole. 2019. "The Metropolitan Museum of Art's Costume Institute Announces Its 2020 Theme: About Time: Fashion and Duration." *Vogue*, 7 November 2019. https://www.vogue.com/article/costume-institute-2020-exhibition-metgala-theme-about-time-fashion-duration.

Piggford, George. 1997. "'Who's That Girl?': Annie Lennox, Woolf's *Orlando*, and Female Camp Androgyny." *Mosaic: An Interdisciplinary Critical Journal* 30, no. 3 (September): 39–58.

Potter, Sally. 2014. *Naked Cinema: Working with Actors*. London: Faber and Faber.

– n.d. "A4 pages, Paper, Typed Notes on Virginia Woolf's Ideas about the Future for Women." Asset ID SPA0000097. SP-ARK: The Sally Potter Archive. http://www.sp-ark.org/itemPage.php?aid=97.

– 1988a. "General Notes on Orlando, Black Printed Text on A4 Paper." Asset IDs SPA0001915-24. 24 October 1988. SP-ARK: The Sally Potter Archive. http://www.sp-ark.org/itemPage.php?aid=1915.

– 1988b. "Black and White, Handwritten, Paper, Rough Draft 1 of Screenplay." Asset IDs SPA0000058–89, SPA00000634–87. 10 November 1988. http://www.sp-ark.org/itemPage.php?aid=58.

– 1988c. "Colour, Handwritten, Paper, Zurich draft, Handwritten, Scene 93-end." Asset IDs SPA0000765–848. 26 November 1988. http://www.sp-ark.org/itemPage.php?aid=765.

– 1989. "Second Draft Script for Orlando. Black Printed Text with Pencil Annotations on A4 Paper, Bound with a Plastic Comb Spine and with

Previous Two Pages Attached with a Paperclip." Asset IDs SPA0001724–914. http://www.sp-ark.org/itemPage.php?aid=1724.

— 1990. "Black and White A4 Computer Printed, Paper, Revised draft of Screenplay." Asset IDs SPA0000008–57, SPA0000001519–723. 1 May 1990. http://www.sp-ark.org/itemPage.php?aid=8.

— 1991. Revised Draft Script with Handwritten Notes and Diagrams in Pencil on Back of Page, A4 White Paper." Asset IDs SPA0001336–518. 1 May 1991. http://www.sp-ark.org/itemPage.php?aid=1336.

— 2019. "Finding Orlando." *Aperture Magazine* 235: 32–9.

Potter, Sally, and Virginia Woolf. 1994. *Orlando*. London: Faber and Faber.

Reich, June L. 1992. "Genderfuck: The Law of the Dildo." Edited by Cheryl Kader and Thomas Piontek. *Discourse* 15, no. 2 (Fall): 112–27.

Reviron-Piégay, Floriane. 2009. "Translating Generic Liberties: *Orlando* on Page and Screen." *Biography* 32, no. 2: 316–39.

Rich, B. Ruby. 2004. "New Queer Cinema." In *New Queer Cinema: A Critical Reader*, edited by Michele Aaron, 15–22. Edinburgh, Scotland: Edinburgh University Press.

Sanders, Julie. 2006. *Adaptation and Appropriation*. London: Routledge.

Sargent, Antwaun, and Mickalene Thomas. 2019. "Orlando Now." *Aperture Magazine* 235: 133–41.

Spenser, Edmund. 1915. *The Faerie Queene*. Edited by Lilian Winstanley. Cambridge: Cambridge University Press.

Stacey, Jackie. 2015. "Crossing Over with Tilda Swinton – The Mistress of 'Flat Affect.'" *International Journal of Politics, Culture, and Society* 28, no. 3 (September): 243–71.

Thomas, Kevin. 1992a. "Jarman Experiments with Tradition in 'Edward' Movies: The Filmmaker Forgoes the Surreal to Make an Accessible, Modern-Dress Version of an Elizabethan Tragedy." *Los Angeles Times*, 4 May 1992.

— 1992b. "MOVIE REVIEW 'Alien' an Engaging Look at Quentin Crisp." *Los Angeles Times*, 9 October 1992.

—1993. "The Mischievous World of Quentin Crisp Movies: The Gay Icon Has Made the Whole Journey from the Outer Suburbs of Ostracism and, at 83, Shows the Wisdom of a Survivor." *Los Angeles Times*, 19 January 1993.

Washington Post. 1993. "Gender Bender; *Orlando* Director Sally Potter Is 'Too Busy' to Be a Woman or a Man." 11 July 1993.

Watkins, Susan. 1998. "Sex Change and Media Change: From Woolf's to Potter's *Orlando*." *Mosaic: An Interdisciplinary Critical Journal* 31, no. 3: 41–59.

Witchel, Alex. 1997. "Nose Up, Chin Up, In a Room of His Own." *New York Times*, 12 June 1997. C:1.

Woolf, Virginia. [1928] 2006. *Orlando: A Biography*. Orlando, FL: Harcourt.

—[1929] 2019. *A Room of One's Own*. London: Penguin Classics.

Filmography

Adaptation., Spike Jonze, USA, 2001, 125 minutes.

Bent, Sean Mathias, UK/Japan, 1997, 105 minutes.

Blue, Derek Jarman, UK, 1993, 79 minutes.

Broken Flowers, Jim Jarmusch, USA/France, 2005, 101 minutes.

Caravaggio, Derek Jarman, UK, 1986, 93 minutes.

The Chronicles of Narnia: The Lion, the Witch and the Wardrobe, Andrew Adamson, UK/USA, 2005, 143 minutes.

Le Confessionnal, Robert Lepage, Canada/France/UK, 1995, 100 minutes.

Edward II, Derek Jarman, UK, 1991, 90 minutes.

An Englishman in New York, Richard Laxton, UK, 2009, 75 minutes.

Gentlemen Prefer Blondes, Howard Hawks, USA, 1953, 91 minutes.

The Gold Diggers, Sally Potter, UK, 1983, 89 minutes.

I Am Love, Luca Guadagnino, Italy, 2009, 120 minutes.

The Living End, Gregg Araki, USA, 1992, 92 minutes.

Man to Man, John Maybury, UK, 1992, 72 minutes.

The Man Who Cried, Sally Potter, UK/France, 2000, 100 minutes.

Moonrise Kingdom, Wes Anderson, USA, 2012, 94 minutes.

My Own Private Idaho, Gus Van Sant, USA, 1991, 105 minutes.

The Naked Civil Servant, Jack Gold, UK, 1975, 78 minutes.

Only Lovers Left Alive, Jim Jarmusch, UK/Germany, 2013, 123 minutes.

Orlando, Sally Potter, UK/Russia/Italy/France/Netherlands, 1992, 94 minutes.

Orlando: The Queer Element, Clay & Diamonds, UK, 2017, live cinema event.

The Party, Sally Potter, UK, 2017, 71 minutes.

Spiderman, Sam Raimi, USA, 2002, 121 minutes.

The Tango Lesson, Sally Potter, Argentina/United Kingdom/France/Germany/Netherlands, 1997, 101 minutes.

Thriller, Sally Potter, UK, 1979, 34 minutes.

We Need to Talk about Kevin, Lynne Ramsay, UK/USA, 2011, 112 minutes.

Yes, Sally Potter, UK/USA, 2004, 100 minutes.

Index